Praise f...

'It's not without pain that our path through life is charted. It's not without hardship that our insight shines to deliver us to enlightenment. Of pain, Dorota has had her fair share. Of hardship, she has had enough to tread the path of the spiritual beings that have come to teach us what we today call happiness.

Dorota's path to healing her wounds came in her ability to love her scars. In this book, she has distilled the essence of what she learned along the way, to help guide you through the process of accepting yourself unconditionally and, in doing so, to learn how self-love is the key to personal growth and a life of fulfilment.

Love is a feeling and self-love is the most elusive of all love. Page by page you will meet yourself, perhaps for the first time, and you will like the one you will meet. Life is a journey, you should take it with those you love and learn to love the one that's always traveling with you — yourself. It will be the biggest gift you will ever receive.'

– Mo Gawdat, former chief business officer for Google X and author of *Solve for Happy*

'I truly recommend you read my dear friend's book, *(Re)Create Yourself*. She has overcome some profound heath conditions and life struggles that have led her to heal herself and to manifest many miracles in her life. It's a true masterpiece on self-love and self-awareness, which are keys to unlocking your true gifts and to create fulfilling relationships. A must-read book to access your true inner power with ease.'

– Dame Marie Diamond,
Feng Shui Master, starring in *The Secret*

'Dorota is one of the powerful, creatively nuanced and compassionate voices of our generation. She has a way of translating relevant and complex philosophies and making them accessible and tangible. Take the time to engage with her work. We need visionaries of the New Earth like Dorota to cultivate and develop cultures and ways of being for the future of humanity.'

– Nicole Gibson, Founder of Love Out Loud and
Former Australian Federal Commissioner of Mental Health

'Dorota's journey is not only inspiring but also empowering. Her openness, honesty and boldness to reveal the most vulnerable parts of herself and her journey allow us to do the same for ourselves. This book teaches us to love, to accept, to own and to transform. I highly recommend it!'

– Jim Kwik, author of *Limitless: Upgrade Your Brain,
Learn Anything Faster, and Unlock Your Exceptional Life*

'If you care deeply about your relationships and seek long-term happiness, then put this book on your required reading list. You will learn to empower yourself, speak your truth and become more confident, but mostly you will be guided on how to connect to your needs, desires and dreams and how to fulfil them. This book will give you the boost you need to believe in yourself.'

– Jason Goldberg, author of *Prison Break*

'It's difficult to describe this book in one word, but I'll give it a shot: transformational. Each section, exercise and story is intended to move you though degrees of self-reflection that allow you to understand both yourself and your relationships better. The outcome is greater peace of mind coupled with a more fulfilling, peaceful and joyful life. Indeed, you're transformed into a more authentic and sincere you. From the poetic to the sublime and practical, this is an enriching, inspiring book. Dive into it for a terrific read. I simply love it.'

– Oz Garcia, pioneer nutritionist, biohacker and author

(RE)CREATE
YOURSELF

(RE)CREATE YOURSELF

Embracing greater self-love
to unleash your potential

Dorota Stańczyk

yellow
kite

First published in Great Britain in 2022 by Yellow Kite
An imprint of Hodder & Stoughton
An Hachette UK company

1

Copyright © 2022 Innerart Ltd

A CIP catalogue record for this title is available from the British Library

Trade Paperback ISBN 978 1 529 37318 9
eBook ISBN 978 1 529 37317 2

Typeset in Sabon MT by Manipal Technologies Limited

Printed and bound in Great Britain by Clays Ltd, Elcograf S.p.A.

Hodder & Stoughton policy is to use papers that are natural, renewable and recyclable products and made from wood grown in sustainable forests. The logging and manufacturing processes are expected to conform to the environmental regulations of the country of origin.

Yellow Kite
Hodder & Stoughton Ltd
Carmelite House
50 Victoria Embankment
London EC4Y 0DZ

www.yellowkitebooks.co.uk

Contents

Life is a dance of the creator.
When you dance become the singer and the song.
Become the writer and the words.
Become the sound and the silence.
Become the instrument and the music.
Become the rhythm and the stillness.
Become the movement and the quiescence.
Become the dancer and the dance.
Become the knower and the known.

Allow your heart to break, to free all the trapped, old grievances and fears, so you can live and love again.

Foreword

There are a lot of things I wish someone had told me when I was young that I didn't come to understand until I was older. *Much* older. This book is full of them.

If I had read *(Re)Create Yourself* forty years ago, it could have saved me a lot of unhappiness, a lot of trial-and-error relationships, and a lot of stalled steps on my search for the best in life.

Dorota Stańczyk has done something quite courageous here. This author has shared her own daily encounters, her own moment-to-moment experience, her own passages through the labyrinth of life, and the realisations they have brought her. She's done this so that, should you notice that you've strayed from the path to your happiness, veered into the woods, and suddenly 'can't see the forest for the trees', you'll discover that the author has gently hung signs everywhere that will lead you out of the thicket.

Authors who are willing to be this vulnerable, this honest, this open about their own early missteps, previous misunderstandings, and ... well, yes, failures ... do not come along very often. I urge you to take advantage of the wonderful wisdom you will find here, for by delving into Dorota's life you may recognise bits of yourself – but just in time to avoid some of the not-so-welcome outcomes she describes.

The invitation on these pages is to recreate yourself in a way that brings you much joy. Savour these recipes from first to last, and make of your life the feast I believe with all my heart that

God intended, and gave us the power to produce, if we only used the tools available to us.

You'll find these tools enumerated from the very first chapter. And don't be fooled into thinking that this book is simply about the author's life. It is about James Thurber's famous 'Everyman', and the value here for you, and for many, could be found to be incalculable.

Thank you, Dorota Stańczyk, for this gift. Herein, insights abound.

Neale Donald Walsch

Introduction

The only way to invest in your future is to create it now.

•

Until you become the source of your happiness, your
journeys will be nothing more than an escape from yourself.

•

Self-love is the courage to show my true self, no matter how
many people can see me.

Love begins with loving oneself. Everything starts there. What is self-love?

For the longest time, I *thought* I could only feel as much love as I was given by others. I believed that others were the only source of love. That I needed to take it from them in order to feel it for myself. So I started to chase after love. The more I got, I believed, the more happy and satisfied I would feel about myself. My well-being was completely dependent on how many people I perceived loved me and supported me. I became the world's foremost people pleaser, thinking that by making everyone around me happy, I would receive some love and appreciation in return. What I realised was that by desiring love this much, I would only push it away. The stronger my desire for love, the stronger the fear became that I would never experience it.

My normal was that love was something hard to get and that I had to deserve it and pay a price for it. It took me a long time to realise that I was fighting for what I was most afraid of.

1

Love terrified me. I believed that love hurts people. I believed that love rejected and pushed away. I didn't know any other way.

I experienced tough love when I was growing up – I learned love through fights, punishment, comparison, jealousy, mental and physical abuse, push-and-pull behaviour and never-ending expectations to be perfect. I experienced lots of pain from the relationships I had in my life and the one I created with myself. In my family there was no demonstration of the feelings of empathy, security, stability, trust or safety. There was no one to give me a right example of how to receive love and most of all, of how to give it.

My hunger for love, and being deserving of it, was so strong that it became the purpose of my life to understand the true source of it. For many years, like a bird trying to swim, I tried to love others without first knowing how to love myself. I didn't even know that self-love existed. How could I ever think that I could love myself if those who were 'supposed' to love me didn't?

There was surely something wrong with me, I thought.

My desperation for the love led me to becoming obsessed with proving to others that I was worth loving. I was fixated on success, career and achievements. I had to be the best at everything I did. Little Miss Perfect, who thought if she knew everything the best, people would love her for it. Wow!

The more I was achieving, the more rejected by others I was feeling. And the more rejected I felt, the more I wanted to hide myself. I started to wear a mask to protect me from the world. A mask through which the little girl inside me screamed constantly, and begged to be seen. I was so convinced that my true self was going to be rejected that I would never show that self to the world. And so I kept rejecting that true self, constantly trying to be someone else.

My love became a neediness, an addiction, a craving for approval. As I was exposed to many relationships with people with an alcohol problem, I developed codependent behaviour; I started to rely excessively – emotionally and psychologically – on my partners. I became a fixer who thought she had to help the entire world.

I started to create in my mind an idea of love. How it should be, how it should be expressed to me and how I should experience it. But what could I know, if I had never really experienced love in its true sense?

Do you know what love really feels like?
Have you ever experienced it, truly?

I thought I knew. I had definitely loved and been loved, but my love was always conditional on what I thought it should look and feel like.

Who am I to tell anyone how they should express their love? I understood that I couldn't force anyone to love me and share love with me in my own way. I could not make anyone guess my needs. I was the only one who could feel into myself and understand what fuels me, what nourishes me, what recharges me. I was the only one who could discover and see my deepest desires and cravings and fulfil them. People often express their love based on how they value themselves. We are not given an instruction manual about how to fulfil someone else's needs based on their individual desires, and we can't expect anyone else to get such a manual to know how to fulfil us. What we need is to create a manual for ourselves by discovering what love means to us. If we learn how to fulfil ourselves, we will know how to guide someone to do the same for us.

Self-love to me is marrying myself – for better and for worse. It is to stop cheating on myself, stop ignoring myself and self-source my own needs and thirsts. To stop punishing and rejecting myself for not fitting into the self-image I had created for myself. It is to let go of that image of who I think I should be. It is to become proud of every single step on my way to self-discovery. It is to give myself a chance to be more than I think I am. It is the courage to show my true self, no matter how many people can see me.

It is to have personal integrity with everything I do and say. It is to trust my own words and actions. It is to take responsibility for what I am creating in my life. It is to become master of what I am feeling, regardless of my circumstances. It is to free myself from my own control, expectations and judgement. It is to be able to hear others without taking anything personally. It is to become a hero, not a victim. It is to share the love I have rather than trying to take it, earn it, win it or deserve it. It is to have enough love for everyone in the room, regardless of how much love I feel from them. It is to trust in the unknown. It is to let go of my deepest fears.

It is to accept that everyone loves differently.

This is what this book is about: understanding love, finally. Love that can't be outsourced, given or earned. Love that can only be generated from within. By accepting that I had no idea what love truly was, I was able to dedicate my life to finding my own answers to it. To create my own definition for love that would never be absent from my life again – because I would become the source of it.

Thanks to the fact that my childhood relationships were far from being 'perfect', I have spent my entire life learning how to navigate through them. Learning how to understand others, myself – and most of all love itself. Learning how to use my experience as a blessing and turning it into my greatest gift.

I was determined to find new systems and ways of thinking that would lead me to attract a model of love that I could never have imagined. I took myself on a path of understanding how our minds work and how our hearts feel.

This book is my own personal path of self-healing. My own personal experience of liberation from self-sabotaging patterns, limiting beliefs, physical manifestations of self-punishment and self-limiting creations. It describes my path from being a lonely, frightened, untrusting and codependent little girl to becoming a woman who taught herself to love herself unconditionally, and who could then open herself to love, and to be loved by others. Who gave herself all her power back.

Before we start, please give yourself some credit for who you are today. For all the things that you have created, fulfilled, experienced and also overcome. For me, overcoming something means letting go of it. Letting go of an idea, dream, vision or expectation.

It means letting go of part of yourself.

Real transformation is giving up one form
before you take on another; it is our
willingness to be nothing for a while.

Be kind and gentle with yourself, and with everything that you still want to create or overcome. It's all about the process.

Can you accept that you might never become anything more than you are here and now? Can you be in love with yourself here and now? That is real freedom. It is liberation from your own expectations about yourself and your own control of how you must be, what you must feel and think and how you must behave. It is the full acceptance of what is.

For me, the goal is the journey. Every moment of my life that I can see, hear, touch and taste. That is the sense of my existence. To experience myself fully, discover my biggest potential and to surrender.

This idea of myself I have created in my mind was ever only stopping me from fully experiencing who I truly was and loving myself unconditionally.

I have chosen to never put any conditions on how and when I will love myself.

Enjoy yourself. Explore yourself. Experience yourself. I wish you a great read!

1

Self-Love

Self-love is not only accepting all parts of yourself, but all
the aspects of yourself mirrored through other people.

•

Before we re-create our world we need to re-create
ourselves and let the world simply reflect our change.

•

Every person in our life carries an aspect of ourselves. Until
we love everyone who reflects the broken pieces of our own
soul, we can never truly love ourselves.

Let's start here, because everything starts from here.

Would you agree that nobody is going to love me just because
I need love? Nobody is going to give me money in order to realise
my dreams. Nobody is going to put me on a plane so I can see
the world. Everything starts from me. I must love, to experience
love. I must realise my dreams, to attract money. I must go out to
the world, in order to see it.

But if I don't have something, I simply can't give it. If I don't
feel secure, I won't be able to reassure anyone. If I don't feel
worthy, I won't invite any abundance into my life. If I don't feel
loveable, I will experience lack of love everywhere. I might look
for hundreds of different things in my external world to fill that
gap without realising that it can be only truly generated from
within.

The love we experience in the first years of life forms the base of our existence. The way we perceive ourselves, and how we are perceived by others, is the result of a long process, going back to not only our childhood but also to the time of being in our mother's womb, feeling and experiencing her emotions, which even then were influencing who we were going to become. The amount and quality of love we get from our parents and kin matters. Family members show us our first example of love. They teach us self-love or lack of it.

They transmit their experiences and the experiences they had with their own family. Some of these are not good experiences to repeat.

Going through a standard education, we learn how to write, count, and use gadgets like computers and cars – yet we are not taught how to use ourselves. Nobody teaches us about intuition, about the information we can obtain from our body, about how we should express our feelings and emotions, or about how to make friends. And they certainly don't teach us the most crucial of lessons: how to love and how to be. Because we do not learn how to understand ourselves – our emotions, desires, needs and boundaries – we learn to ignore them. Therefore we start to appease ourselves blindly with external things. We disconnect from ourselves, numbing the discomfort created by misalignment.

I realised that for many years I had thought I was feeling, but I was not in fact feeling at all. Instead I was numbing the sensations in my body, not letting them speak up or trying to understand them. The more I tried to control and suppress my emotions, the more discomfort I would feel. But more uncomfortable than the feelings was my own rejection and judgement of them.

This disconnection from my feelings created an illusory impression that those feelings didn't depend on me, almost as if they were not mine. I started to believe that the feelings I felt depended on my external world and other people. I would blame everything around me for what I was experiencing within. I assumed that the emptiness and loneliness inside me was due to the fact that I didn't receive enough love from others.

So I started to chase love to 'fix' myself. Since I didn't know what love really was, I created this idea in my head of an ideal love and an ideal partner. That very carefully crafted and idealised image of how he should be. Affectionate, generous, open, kind. He had to fulfil every condition that I couldn't fulfil for myself. He had to save me from myself. What a job!

For the longest time I wasn't in a relationship with another person but with my own idea of them. I tried to cast people around me in the roles I wanted them to play. My filters were enabling me to see only my own twisted, mostly not favourable, interpretations of the other person's actions.

The more incompatible the person was with my vision, the more frustrated and obsessed by changing him I became. And the more specific my vision became, the more painful and difficult my separation from it.

I assumed I knew what was right for me and what would make me happy; therefore I felt baffled and disappointed. Nobody was able to fill me with the thing I lacked.

I framed not only how the other should be but also how I myself should be. I wanted to control how people would perceive me because I was too afraid of what they might see in me if I showed them my true self.

Terrified by the idea of being judged by others, I started to hide behind an image I created. A vision that I would need to prove and fight for constantly. A mask that made me lose many friends – slowly, I was forgetting and denying who I truly was.

My idea of myself imprisoned me and limited my access to my true self. Instead of discovering and experiencing myself, I would spend all my energy on trying to maintain and carry this image. I preferred to put myself in some sort of frame of adjectives and stay loyal to this frame, using it also as an excuse for my unwillingness to change or show up.

'This is who I am,' I would say, 'Accept it,' eventually forgetting that the entire mask was built on self-rejection, self-judgement, shame for who I was and guilt for the experiences I went through.

Do you really accept who you are? Do you accept yourself when you feel sadness and disappointment or when you think you are not 'good' enough? Do you accept yourself when you feel guilty or ashamed, or do you try to escape that feeling as soon as you can and change yourself? Do you punish yourself for not being who you think you should be, and not doing what you think you should do? I did. I would always beat myself up for not living up to my own expectations.

I tried to escape and hide who I was and especially what I felt, for the longest time. I realised that there is nothing more uncomfortable than a resistance to feeling whatever is there to be felt. This feeling of resistance was almost more uncomfortable than what I was trying to escape from in the first place. The desire to be somewhere else and to feel something else pushed me to look for other states of mind. Grasping those other states of mind was nothing more than a way to experience freedom from myself for a moment.

For many years, I avoided feeling or thinking; I used spirituality to do this, rather than using it to find what was really going on deep down in my heart. Relationships became a constant chase after 'otherness'. I was constantly looking for something different from the present moment.

For the first few months of every new relationship, everything always seemed right. Novelty, adventure and excitement gave me the momentary illusion of change, but I would soon realise that the void I always had inside me had appeared again. I would do anything not to feel that void. I would change partners, jobs, homes, cities, projects. I travelled more, worked more, bought more, searched more.

But if I didn't accept myself for who I truly was and how I felt, how could other people ever accept me? I realised that I was my own worst enemy. When I fell, I punished myself for falling. When I won, I thought I didn't deserve it. When people hurt me, I convinced myself that it was my fault. I could be so kind to others and so unkind to myself.

What would you say to your friend: *Stop being sad!*
***What is wrong with you?* No. You would say:**
Hey, I love you. Everything will be all right. You are amazing.

As Jamie Catto points out, how liberating it would be to say: *I am sad today and I love myself with this sadness. I didn't achieve my goal and I love myself anyway.*[1]

We should treat ourselves how we want to be treated by others. The relationships we have with people in our life mirror the relationship we have with ourselves.

People will only ever treat us according
to how we treat ourselves.

Every person I encountered along my way was exactly the right person. They were the perfect reflection of who I was at that moment. I could not always recognise my own visage in the other, but I know now that it was always there to point out who I was. Every relationship reflected back at me what I had to see, learn, heal, overcome or accept. So this is why we must love our enemies. Because every person in our life carries an aspect of ourselves. Until we love everyone who reflects the broken pieces of our own soul, we can never truly love ourselves.

This process lasts our whole lifetime. Through the relationships and the experiences we create, we learn who we are. That is why every relationship is precious; it helps us to know ourselves better.

Self-love is about opening our doors and windows to the world, showing ourselves truly without any judgement, shame or guilt. It is acknowledging all the wounds and welcoming all the emotions that have been suppressed for a long time inside ourselves. It is being gentle and kind to ourselves no matter how we feel. It is becoming our own best friend no matter what. It is focusing on building a connection rather than an image. It is feeling whole even when there is no one around. It is feeling seen when no one is looking. It is having the courage to wake up every day and create who we are.

Into-me-I-see

I would like you to buy a nice workbook for this exercise (and for the many more to come in this book). Your personal transformational book that we will create during this journey together.

We have a tendency to focus on the negative, very rarely acknowledging or even recognising the positives. This is likely a result of evolution; in early human history, paying attention to dangerous and negative things – threats – was literally a matter of survival. Neuroscientific study has shown that there is greater neural processing in the brain in response to negative stimuli than positive.[2] And we do the same with ourselves.

So your first task is to write a list of things you like about yourself and read it every morning after waking up. You can keep the list next to your mirror in the bathroom or next to your coffee machine.

You could write down things about your talents, your unique gifts, your strengths, your character, your taste, your way of being or your wisdom. Keep adding new things to this list as you discover them. Keep discovering yourself and seeing yourself through the lenses of gratitude and appreciation.

When you change the way you look at yourself and see yourself in a new light, your whole experience of life will change too.

So write down on a sheet from your new book everything that you like about yourself. Look at it every day and remind yourself how amazing you are.

2

Take Off Your Mask

Once you taste how good it feels to actually be you and
to allow people to see you, there is no way back
to carrying the heavy masks of self-protection.

•

There is a big difference between
thinking who you are and knowing who you are.
When you know who you are,
no negative gesture, word or behaviour from
another person can ever change your sense of yourself.

•

There comes a time when you must un-become
everything you are, in order to be.
You must undress, unlearn, unravel and unframe the
ideas, thought forms and beliefs you have accepted
about who you are in order to create yourself anew.

How Many Masks Do You Have?

The first step to removing your mask is to realise that your mask exists. The question isn't whether you have a mask, but how many?

Have you ever truly considered what it is you want people to think about you? What lengths have you gone to in order to create that impression? Without desire to influence anyone, there is no need to control and adapt our behaviour. Would you agree?

For many years what others thought about me was much more important than what I was thinking about myself. My own opinion didn't matter unless it was approved by others. I became what I thought others thought of me.

I realised that every time I tried to control other people's feelings and opinion about me I unconsciously manipulated my behaviour. Every time I tried to guess what they were thinking or feeling, I wasn't behaving naturally. I wasn't being myself. I was adapting the posture of someone who I thought they wanted me to be. I wanted to satisfy them or be more likeable to deserve their love. I was like a chameleon who could adapt to any circumstances and play any role. I looked like someone who had this big personality, originality and individuality, but deep inside I was a little girl who wanted people to like her.

On the other hand, I was like a puppet with dangling strings that anyone could pull. Every breeze blew me in every direction. I reacted exaggeratedly to everything. My whole life was one big reaction to the desires, successes, failures, problems, behaviours, thoughts, feelings of others (as Melody Beattie neatly describes in her book *Codependent No More*).[3] While I was reacting to what they could feel, think or do I was losing my ability to think, feel or behave in the best way for me. All my actions and behaviours were filtered by what I thought others thought or felt. It was real codependency.

I believe that every time we don't behave as if nobody was watching or listening, we change who we are. Instead of being faithful to ourselves we manipulate our behaviours, actions and words to try to get the reaction we want from others.

15

In my experience we only wear masks when we don't know how to stand up for who we truly are – or, worse still, when we hate who we truly are and we want to hide it. Wearing masks is often rooted in self-rejection, low self-esteem, fear, self-judgement or shame in ourselves.

Masks are, after rationalisation and projection, one of the unconscious mind's most beloved techniques for repressing parts of ourselves. Repression creates what is called 'cognitive dissonance': in the field of psychology, mental discomfort or psychological stress experienced by a person who simultaneously holds two or more contradictory beliefs, ideas or values.[4]

In other words, it is a disconnect between who we 'think' we are and who we 'actually' are. We create so many social masks, which we wear on a daily basis to fit in, that after a while we don't know any more who we truly are.

I started to wear my first mask when I started school. I was so desperate for love and to deserve love that I tried to please everyone. I was so convinced that who I was was not enough that I started to behave in the way I thought the other children expected me to. It was of course a creation of my own imagination – how could I possibly know what others wanted from me without them telling me?

This adopted posture to gain friends was, as you can imagine, far from natural, confident or funny. It was awkward. And everyone can feel when there is someone awkward in the room!

I started to be rejected and bullied for being too nice to people, for being a people pleaser. My greatest fear – of rejection – would materialise on a daily basis. Kids hated me. I will never forget the time when the entire classroom screamed out loud: *Get rid of Dorota!*

My beloved teacher, with compassionate tears in her eyes, looked at me sadly with no words. I completely lost faith in myself. So I resolved instead to pretend that I had it.

I decided that I had to be stronger, more powerful and more original. I started to think more carefully about what to say, how to behave, how to look. I started to provoke, deliberately stand out and invite attention. The mask was getting thicker. I was hiding myself more and more deeply behind my image, projects, appearance and my work as an artist. The more vulnerable I was feeling inside, the more self-confident I wanted to look outside. I started becoming what I was pretending to be: bold, independent, provocative. I became convinced that I knew exactly who I was. Surely someone so expressive and noticeable must have a deep sense of self?

But did I really know who I was? Was everything I believed about myself true? And what did I really believe about myself?

False Beliefs

Many years passed and I've learned to perfectly hide my insecurities. I became my own best piece of work. I created a strong, resilient, thick image of myself that was hiding and protecting that little frightened girl I once was. I started to wear very unconventional clothes, shaved half of my head and tattooed half of my body. I not only became hard to approach but I also distanced myself from people. My career grew. But the more successful I was becoming, the more I was pushing people away, afraid of them rejecting me.

I started to work with big brands and successful companies all around the world. I was both attending and co-creating global transformational events and I was surrounded by many people of influence. One day at a conference, I was asked to give a short speech in front of almost a thousand people. I couldn't sleep the night before, from the stress of imagining being on stage. I knew everyone thought of me as someone who would not have any problem with public speaking, but the truth was that when I had to present myself to a bigger group of people or do a presentation for colleagues, I felt completely paralysed and my hands would shake. Of course, I hid my shyness; I had to be seen as the strong, inspirational woman I was pretending to be. But all I really wanted was to run away and hide.

I was convinced I was no good on stage. I would repeat to myself how bad a speaker I was.

The fear became unbearable and I knew that I had to do it. Not really for the speech, but to overcome the fear itself. As I was walking towards the stage that day I couldn't breathe, my heart was beating fast and the world was spinning. What was wrong with me? Other people didn't seem to get so stressed.

When I was finally standing in front of all those people, something unexpected happened: all my fear was suddenly gone. I realised that I had been more afraid of the idea of being afraid than of what was actually going to happen.

Hundreds of images passed through my mind, images of me as a little girl who loved performing, singing, dancing, reciting poetry. What happened to that confident girl I was back then? Why had I had to pretend to be self-confident all this time, rather than just remaining self-confident like I used to be? Like we all used to be. When you watch kids playing, they don't care what others think, they don't put the handbrake on their self-expression, they don't limit their imagination or creativity; most of all, they don't suspend their access to joy.

That moment was crucial. Not because I had overcome fear per se, but because I realised that perhaps many more things I had believed about myself were simply not true. Without trying, there was so many things I hadn't even given myself a chance of exploring, out of simple fear of not being good at it. We all are conditioned to believe many things through our experiences and sometimes one tiny comment from someone can destroy our self-confidence to try what we secretly dream about. The joy I have received through putting myself out there, on that stage, and sharing my thoughts with people about the idea of marrying ourselves, for better or worse, was way more important than if I was good at it or not. I took the very first step to show myself, to share a piece of my soul, the first step that would change my life for ever. Because once you taste how good it feels to actually be you and to allow people to see you, there is no way back to carrying the heavy masks of self-protection.

When we start to live according to our deepest alignment with who we truly are, we can finally emerge in our reality.

How many other false beliefs did I have? Did I really know who I was? I wasn't so sure any more. I had learned to hide myself so early in life that I never gave myself a chance to discover myself fully. I rejected myself way before others rejected me.

My first talk attracted hundreds of thousands of views in its first week. That year I was invited to speak on more than ten different international stages, including TEDx. My life was changed for ever by one brave decision to go beyond what I thought about myself. Beyond my fear. After my video was shared I decided to finish writing this book, which I had started a few years earlier, even though I didn't have a publisher and didn't know how I would get it out there. Three weeks after I had finished the last chapter, the person who is now my publisher contacted me out of nowhere. She explained that she had seen my video online and asked me if I would be interested in publishing a book on self-love...!

How many false beliefs do you have about yourself?
How many of them are actually serving you?
How many of them are you ready to let go of?

I realised that I could only free myself if I truly let go of my reaction to other people's behaviours and my own interpretation of it. It is not the fear of other people's judgement that I was the most afraid of, but rather my own judgement on myself, which I assumed people might share. The judgement of others can't harm us if we don't judge ourselves.

I realised that every time I named myself, I framed myself – every time I thought to myself, 'I am not good at something,' 'I am shy' 'I don't speak well enough' 'I can't do it', I put around myself an invisible wall that would limit me. Let's be careful with all the frames we put around ourselves. Every repeated word becomes a belief we then hold on to. Some of them are positive but some are negative. Some of them are conscious and some of them, programmed into our psyche by negative criticism from others when we were young, can become unconscious.

Conscious and unconscious beliefs are contradictory. We want to believe one thing about ourselves without realising that we operate from the position of believing the opposite thing.

When we are limited by our beliefs, we doom ourselves to rove around searching for happiness and fulfilment rather than creating it for ourselves.

One day I was participating in a workshop and we were asked to do a meta-perception exercise. I had to imagine that I was a man and describe how I was perceiving myself from that point of view. I was shocked by what I discovered. I looked at myself and saw myself almost as a sculpture that people should admire from afar but should not touch. Inaccessible, distant, frozen. Wow! This was how, unconsciously, I thought men perceived me. Guess what kind of man would be attracted to someone like that?

Then I had to look at myself from the perspective of being a woman. I saw myself as cold, serious, closed, secretive.

Seriously? I always thought I was the most playful, honest, funny, childlike girl on Earth! But that was not how I subconsciously believed the woman perceived me! What reality would create this kind of belief?

Thanks to this exercise, probably for the very first time I realised I was wearing masks. Different masks for different situations and circumstances. Those masks were a barrier separating me not only from other people, but also – and mostly – from myself.

I had to accept that I was a sensitive, hurt, timid little girl who would not truly let anyone in, rather than the strong, independent woman I thought myself to be. When I opened my arms to this little girl, not only did I heal physically but I also started to discover myself again. Through accepting and integrating all the negative (in my eyes) parts of myself, I could finally notice and appreciate the good ones.

A philosopher and sociologist, Charles Horton Cooley, said: 'I am not who you think I am; I am not who I think I am; I am who

I think you think I am.'[5] We often judge other people by what we think they think of us. If we think others perceive us in a positive way, we are more likely to invest in those relationships. If we think the other person has a negative perception of us, we will more likely push that person away. This is because we will do anything to protect that idea of ourselves we have created. But it is just an idea. There is a big difference between thinking who you are and knowing who you are.

When you know who you are, no negative gesture, word or behaviour from another person can ever change your sense of yourself.

Coming back to Cooley, it doesn't matter what we think about a person, it matters how we feel about ourselves when we are with them. But what if we could create a stable sense of who we are that would be completely independent to what others might think of us? Wouldn't that be a real freedom?

Feeling It

Often what influences how people feel about us is actually how we feel about ourselves. People's liking or disliking us is rarely rational; rather, it's energetic. We 'vibe' – whether well or not – with the other person.

When we first meet someone, our field will react to their field, causing certain feelings. We can use these feelings, or ignore and suppress them. They are there in order to guide us. They are our sixth sense, and they can be developed so that we can have better 'vibes' or connections with other people.

22

Everybody feels other people's energy, but not everybody can recognise it and process the information. Sometimes we feel something weird but we can't define it, and so end up rationalising it. But, if there is someone in the room who is angry, upset or awkward, we always feel it, don't we? Our energy sends information to our surroundings about our internal state. If I am sad, even if I put a smile on my face, people will sense that there's something wrong. Jamie Catto writes in his book, *Insanely Gifted*, that there is something uncomfortable or even claustrophobic when we are in the vicinity of a person who suppresses their feelings. We feel discomfort because the person is wearing a mask and so in a way is editing themself.

C. G. Jung, the famous psychiatrist and psychoanalyst who founded analytical psychology, said that if we discover what is behind the mask we wear during the day and accept all the flaws and ugliness that can be found in our shadow, our emotions will become uninhibited, the instinct will be stronger and perception wider.

There is no faster way to reveal the masks we are wearing and hiding behind than through the eyes of another person.

Therefore, it is not strange that we turn away from relationships. We fear them, we do not trust them, we reject or destroy them, because we are trying to maintain our vision of ourselves. But what we're actually afraid of is the fear of confronting ourselves. This fear shows up as a judgemental little voice in our mind that separates us from who we really are; it separates us from our potential. This little voice can be nasty, irrational, confusing, disempowering. It is programmed to think based on what we have been taught, just like an AI that learns from examples of acts and behaviours. But that little voice is not who we truly are. Remember, our soul never screams, it only whispers. It doesn't

23

think, it feels. And we can only hear it when we overcome that voice in our head and go beyond it.

> In order to hear, we need to keep quiet.
> In order to listen, we need to silence our mind.

As Wayne Dyer says, transformation literally means going beyond your form.

By doing this, we open up new possibilities of creation and we give ourselves a chance to truly experience our powers. Our entire reality is an extension of who we are. It is constant feedback about where we are at.

> Things don't happen to you, they
> don't happen for you, they happen from you.

By discovering and re-creating yourself you gain full control of your life. All the negative experiences in your life come from the barriers you have created against yourself. Drop them. Today.

Reinventing Who We Are

Only when we are truly open to see absolutely everything about ourselves will we be free to choose and decide who we would like to be. We will be ready to re-create ourselves anew. We will be ready to reinvent who we are.

Reinventing who we are is the hardest and the scariest thing in the world. It is much easier to just follow whatever comes to us, whatever was chosen for us, whatever was given to us, whatever has come our way. *What am I supposed to do with my life? What am I made for? What am I here for? What is my destiny?* we often ask. But what is destiny? It is the path that has been defined, shaped, directed, specified. But shaped by who? By what? Contracts, agreements, bonds, commitments, promises, debts... By the decisions and actions of ourselves and others that sometimes that we are not even aware of. This path we blindly follow without questioning or realising that one decision made at one point in time might be defining the course of our life, is this destiny?

And what if we suddenly awake? If we start to look around, and by free choice end, cut, resolve, let go of and free ourselves from everything that was guiding our life. What is left? Space, Void, Silence, Unknown, Stillness. Nothing is pushing or pulling us any more. We become free.

And what's left is pure Creation. The only place we can experience ourselves as Creator. Becoming Creator means facing the unknown. Facing the void, the stillness, the silence, space. And using it to create our own voice, our own sound, our own form, our own expression.

And it can be the most confusing moment ever. Because we are so used to hearing that little voice pushing or pulling us in different directions that suddenly when that little voice disappears and there is nothing but space, we panic. We don't know how to take over.

It is so much easier to be told what to do or to be shown where to go rather than to create it yourself. We don't know how to create. We wait for something to happen in order to act. But it is acting that will create something.

At this moment, when we are truly ready to create, it feels as if the world has abandoned us. It feels as if the world has stopped. But it is just standing still and waiting for us to make a move. Giving us a lot of space to create.

It's saying: It's up to you now. You are ready. You don't need me to guide you any more. You can choose to create whatever you want. So, go ahead. Dive into your imagination.

I won't tell you any more who to be, it's saying; I want YOU to tell ME who you are so I can shape your whole reality according to that.

Choose to create yourself as if nothing was pulling or pushing you in any direction any more. From the place of a pure source. Become a Creator of your life. Today.

In the time of unknowingness, when nothing can be seen, a new life is being created. It is under cover of darkness when the seed can crack open and take root. It is under cover of darkness when your soul can grow into a new life.

I invite you to unlearn, to unravel and to unframe the ideas, thought forms and beliefs you have accepted about who you are, and discover those that are hiding behind your mask, the ones that shape your reality. True self-expression, with the willingness to be vulnerable, open and courageous, is the key to a deepening of the connection, the love and the trust in ourselves and others.

We are all stones, yet if we let the light move through us, we will become diamonds. Then, we reveal the beauty and treasure we have inside. How can we let the light move through us? By cracking the walls we have built around ourselves. By expressing who we really are and by doing the best we can do.

Sometimes, it is by allowing our heart to break once more, to free all the trapped grievances and fears, so we can live and love again.

The light enters when we become open to our potential and allow the voice of our soul to speak through us. When we express ourselves, showing our gifts, we unite with the highest form of our existence. Lack of self-love is nothing else but constant rejection of who we truly are. Not only the parts of ourselves that are in our eyes negative, but also the great parts.

Shine and brighten everything around you. Reveal yourself. Stop hiding your true nature.

Eventually, others will see themselves in you.

Butterfly

This exercise will reveal some of the foundational beliefs you hold about yourself, conscious and unconscious. It might bring up some negative feelings and sensations in your body, but these are just proof that you are doing this work right. Keep in mind that everything that becomes part of your awareness can't control you any more, it can only set you free.

With your workbook or journal, sit in a quiet space by yourself. Think about the questions below very carefully, then write down your answers.

- What do you say about yourself to yourself and to others?
- What do you think others think of you?
- What opinions do you have about yourself?
- Are those beliefs genuinely yours, or have people told them to you, or have you created them yourself?
- What experiences have created those beliefs?
- Are your beliefs empowering, or rather limiting?
- Do they move you at a deep level or are they holding you back?
- Are these beliefs the ones you would like to keep?

3

Behind the Fear of Rejection

*What you do to yourself, people will do to
you to reflect your attitude towards yourself.*

•

*In my experience, it is much more painful to be
rejected for who you are not than for who you truly are.*

How Afraid Of Rejection Are You?

I was always afraid of rejection. It all started when I was
rejected by my brother when I was little. And I don't just
mean a typical sibling conflict. I didn't even have my brother's
phone number for over twenty-eight years. I can't explain why
we didn't bond; perhaps our parents started to give me more
attention than him and he felt rejected. Or perhaps he simply
didn't like me; but it was a very hard relationship for me for
many, many years.

Because of constantly feeling pushed away and unwanted, I
created a belief that I was not loveable. That belief would create
my whole experience of my reality. I would keep retraumatising myself by attracting a great rejection to my life to prove to
myself that my belief was real. It was easier to agree on an idea
of myself and simply go with 'here I go again' than to question
my entire experience of life.

In order to protect myself I would put up all possible defences.
I would reject before being rejected, I would provoke people to

reject me so it happened sooner rather than later and I didn't have to wait for it, or I would numb myself completely. I would stop letting people in, I would never fully open up or get too attached, always being prepared for anyone to leave my life tomorrow. There was a part of me that I would never reveal. A secret I was hiding. A great secret of who I truly was. After some time, I forgot what the secret was. I only knew that I had to hide and protect something.

When we protect ourselves from rejection, we lock ourselves inside a little invisible house. We close the door and all the windows. We feel safe. No one can get in but we can't get out either. We can't really give or receive. Nothing can flow through the walls. Everything that tries to come to us has to knock many times before we hear it. We even forget after a while how to open the door.

I stayed locked up for years. I started to dream about someone coming and finding me. Discovering me. Seeing me. I wanted to come out of my cave to shine in the light of the sun. But how could I get out without the key?

If your greatest desire is to be seen for who you are, it means that you are hiding yourself. If you are hiding yourself it means you are rejecting parts of yourself you don't want to reveal. You create social masks so you will not be rejected by others – for the very same reasons for which you have rejected yourself: those things you are the most ashamed about.

If you wear a mask, you are never rejected for who you are, but for who you are NOT.

So clever!

I asked myself one day: What is more uncomfortable, hiding and rejecting myself all the time or being rejected for who I am from time to time?

I realised that my greatest pain didn't come from rejection from others but from my own rejection of myself. There is nothing more uncomfortable than to keep rejecting yourself. And if you are not showing who you truly are at every moment, that means you are rejecting yourself constantly. There is nothing more beautiful than someone being true and vulnerable.

A man revealing to a woman how stressed he is in her presence. A woman revealing to a man how nervous she is before their first date. How many couples haven't been created because we were NOT who we are, unable to communicate our vulnerability and truth? How many friendships have been sacrificed because we were too afraid to communicate with each other honestly?

If you show who you are and people reject you, at least they have rejected you for who you truly are. But if they reject you for who you are not it will always cause you great pain.

You are going to save so much time by being YOU. Now and at every moment. Communicate what you think and feel. Be truthful to others but, most importantly, to yourself. Express yourself fully, with all the uniqueness you have in you. You might think that this is going to make you separate, but the truth is that it is going to reunite you – with yourself. And when you are reunited with yourself, you can truly reunite with others. When I started to show who I am my fear of rejection dissolved.

There is nothing in this world, external or internal,
that doesn't come from you. And you should
never reject something that is yours.

As long as you keep rejecting yourself, you won't be able to let go of the fear of being rejected, which will bear fruit by attracting even more rejection into your life. As long as you keep rejecting yourself, others will keep rejecting you. So simply how you are with yourself will become your own experience of life, as life is nothing else but an extension of you. Only true self-love and acceptance will set you free from the fear of other people's judgement.

And yes, it might happen that you will be rejected for who you truly are, but in my experience, it is much more painful to be rejected for who you are NOT than for who you are.

If you run away from being you, you can't create anything that comes from you; you will create the very experience that is NOT coming from who you truly are and therefore it won't serve your greatest good. The situations you will create, the people who you will attract, the work you will produce won't be in alignment with your true self and it will only bring you even more misalignment in your life. When you are not acting from your truest self, not only do you take away from yourself the possibility to experience this life through you, you also limit the possibilities for the world to witness your great unique self.

Letting Go

As we have seen, the first step to overcoming fear of rejection from others is never to reject or try to escape something that is yours. Practising this exercise for just five minutes can make a big difference in how you feel.

When you feel an uncomfortable emotion in your body, don't do anything to try to change it or escape it. Lie down on your bed or somewhere comfortable with your hands facing upwards, close your eyes and take a deep breath.

Feel where the uncomfortable emotion is in your body, what colour it is, what shape, what the physical sensation is.

Then breathe into it and say out loud if you can: Thank you, I love you, I let go. Imagine you are falling down and all those emotions are slowly dissolving from your body. Imagine you are letting go of everything that holds you back.

If it helps, you can play gentle music while going through this process.

If you ever feel an uncomfortable emotion somewhere where you can't lie down, simply smile and say to yourself: *I feel anger and I love myself with this anger* or *I feel sadness and I love myself with this sadness* or whichever uncomfortable emotion you are feeling. Feel compassion for whatever you are feeling as experiencing emotions is simply a part of being a human.

Facing Rejection

If you are afraid of rejection, ask yourself: Are you showing who you truly are? What are you rejecting in yourself? Is there anything you are ashamed of? Can you stand up for who you truly are?

4

Facing Your Shadow

Sometimes it is easier to know who we
are if we contrast it with who we are not.
After all – the stars shine brighter at night.

•

We can't witness how much we've evolved
without seeing our reflection in our external
reality and another person, our mirror.

Can you think of a time when you did something that was 'out of character' for you?

Did you consider those to be 'anomalies'? What if I told you that everything you rejected about yourself in that moment was exactly who you are, but you simply refuse to see it?

One day, my mother told me imperiously to do something. I refused politely, because I considered it irrelevant and in order to do it, I would have to give up other activities. She persisted. Her tone was demanding. Eventually, I could not stand it any longer and I exploded. I shouted and couldn't calm down. I couldn't stand being bossed around. I was not a child. I had to go out of the house to cool down. Then I asked myself a question: 'Where are these emotions coming from?' The answer was that it was not my mum who was responsible for my emotions but my own self reflecting back from her.

Then I asked what I could blame her for. The answer was: she was being controlling, bossy and authoritative. I understood that my tears were not over *her* control, bossiness and sense of authority but mine. Whatever I was pointing out in her, I was refusing to see in myself. I projected on to her my own shadow. I saw how much I would always try to control myself; I would boss myself around and I would try to always meet my own expectations. What's worse, without realising it, I would do the same with others.

This was how I treated myself? In the past, I would have felt guilty for such behaviour, such release of emotions and lack of control. Now, however, I understood that it was a blessing for me. A kind of purification. A scream of my soul, loud enough that I could hear it.

I understood that everything that irritates us about others is in fact a reflection of our own flaws that we are trying to reject. My resentment had nothing to do with my mother, who simply showed me the truth about myself.

Such moments of confrontation, when we 'fly off the handle', make us reveal our true colours. These moments open us to the truth. They open us to our shadow.

The Shadow: Our 'Dark Side'

The shadow is a psychological term for everything we can't see in ourselves. In his book *Psychology and Religion* Jung says:

Everyone carries a shadow, and the less it is embodied in the individual's conscious life, the blacker and denser it is. If an inferiority is conscious, one always has a chance to correct it. Furthermore, it is constantly in contact with other interests, so that it is continually subjected to modifications. But if it is repressed and isolated from consciousness, it never gets corrected.[6]

It is much easier to recognise another's shadow than our own. We struggle to acknowledge the 'dark side' of our personality, as it consists chiefly of primitive, negative emotions and impulses like rage, envy, greed, selfishness, desire and striving for power. Everything we deny, judge, reject or perceive as unacceptable or wrong in ourselves, or disidentify with, becomes part of the shadow.

In order to protect our self-image from anything unflattering or unfamiliar we do many different things and go to great lengths. We divorce ourselves from anything that doesn't get acceptance or approval from our environment, including our parents, teachers, family, friends – but mostly ourselves. Suppressed shadows might cause social anxiety, deviant sexual behaviour, limiting beliefs, uncontrollable anger, arrogance and haughtiness, problems getting along with people or neuroticism. Scott Jeffrey, founder of CEOsage, a transformational leadership agency, talks about this in his article 'Shadow Work'.[7]

He also explains that in order to prevent the mental discomfort experienced when we simultaneously hold two or more contradictory beliefs, ideas or values, our mind develops and uses the techniques of rationalisation, social masks and projection. He elaborates that in psychology, projection is the act of ascribing to other people character traits that in fact are our own. Things that you do not recognise in yourself and so criticise in others. As I did when I had that argument with my mother.

Rationalisation is justification of certain acts or behaviours in certain situations. Social masks, as we have seen, are the disguises that we wear on a daily basis to fit in. All of these are ways in which we repress our shadow selves. All of those techniques are defence mechanisms. We do it to keep us safe and in the 'known'.

Jamie Catto also talks about projection and says that projection of our shadow makes our entire world a replica of our unknown, hidden face.[8] Shadows are unexpressed parts of us, 'edited' versions of ourselves.

Reflections of Ourselves

The only part of ourselves we cannot see is our face. It is hugely important because it represents our identity; but the only way to see our own face is in the mirror. In life, the other person is such a mirror. How we perceive that person and what we see in him/her depends on our attitude to ourselves. Every person is perceived differently by everyone else; there are as many opinions on us as there are people we know, for they all see different aspects of themselves in us. The picture that will eventually develop from all these aspects will reflect what is going on inside us.

The theory makes even more sense when we understand that we choose the people we are surrounded by. Everything we see in those people is nothing but our own reflection. Energy attracts like energy. If you often encounter people who are unfaithful or disloyal, for example, it's worthwhile checking in with yourself to think about in which ways you've been unfaithful or disloyal towards them or towards yourself. If you constantly meet greedy people, examine to what extent it refers to you yourself. Are you dishonest? Do you attract dishonesty through your thoughts, feelings or experiences about dishonest people?

The mirror effect is a philosophical concept similar to projection that suggests that everything we see in another person is nothing but a reflection of ourselves and our emotions. It can be positive as well as negative; Michel Odoul writes in his book *What Your Aches and Pains Are Telling You,* that if we like a particular feature in someone, it is probably also a trait of our own that we, for some reason, are not able to notice or express.[9]

In psychology this is called the 'positive shadow'. In *How to Be An Adult*, psychologist David Richo explains:

> To integrate the positive Shadow is to acknowledge our own untapped potential behind the awe we have of others. We begin to acknowledge and to release from within ourselves the very talents and qualities we admired in others.[10]

Another term we can use for our *positive shadow* is inner gold. This is the hidden potential, the unseen and unrecognised unique attributes we were gifted with that will touch us when we see them expressed in others. Think about someone you admire, perhaps someone for whom you have feelings of awe. What is it you like about them? Maybe their courage, their conviction, their charisma, their intelligence, their creativity, their talent? Maybe their kindness, their generosity, their style or their cooking skills. The stronger your feeling of awe, the more this indicates that you are holding those very qualities inside yourself; they are just perhaps not yet fully recognised or expressed.

Synchronicity

We perceive and are attracted to things that concern ourselves and vice versa. That is the way the universe is constructed. When we decide to buy a particular make of a car, we suddenly start seeing those cars everywhere. It's not because there are suddenly more cars of that kind on the roads; it's due to the fact that we now have that kind of car in our minds and so we notice them more easily.

In the same way as with cars – our thoughts, conscious and subconscious – lead us to meet people who reflect where we are at and create situations that represent our current state of being. When we wish to change or discover something in ourselves, some information, a clue or a solution often arises out of meeting (who we think are) random people, hearing a radio broadcast or reading an article. Jung called this 'synchronicity'. It's our external reality constantly communicating with us about our inner world so we can keep experiencing ourselves through it.

The challenge is to recognise those signs and clues that are offered at many moments in order for us to see ourselves. Nothing in this life is accidental. Everything is a reflection of where we are at. We can't witness how much we've evolved without seeing our reflection in our external reality and in another person, our mirror.

Shadows... and Light

Jung says in *Psychology and Alchemy*: 'There is no light without shadow and no psychic wholeness without imperfection.'[11]

In other words, facing and working on our shadow will pay off. It will lead to unity, integration and wholeness within ourselves. With shadow work, we can liberate a tremendous reservoir of energy that we have previously been unconsciously expending on protecting ourselves. We will experience much more balance in our life, unleash great creativity, self-expression, integrity, fulfilment and joy. Tibetan Buddhists believe that our enemies, those who cause us the most suffering, are our greatest teachers because they push us forward.

Every person we meet on our path is the right person because we always attract the person who will help us uncover the truth concerning ourselves. Reclaiming our projections and thereby facing our shadow – good and bad – is the only way to real liberation. By this process we improve all our relationships; we are no longer triggered by others and instead can view other people with much more compassion. Our perception of the world gets clearer, as we no longer see the world through a cracked or cloudy lens. We no longer drag around an invisible bag of repressed and suppressed unconscious self-perceptions. We gain energy and boost our physical health and well-being. With shadow work, we liberate a tremendous reservoir of energy we were unconsciously investing in protecting ourselves. Shadow work leads to unity, integration and wholeness within ourselves but most importantly, it leads to self-love. If you can recognise, accept, own and love the rejected parts of yourself, you will not only become more complete with who you are, but you will also give yourself the freedom to consciously re-create yourself.

The Mirror

List three errors that you frequently observe in others. What don't you like about them? Maybe their selfishness, their cluelessness, their nastiness, their inauthenticity.

Example: I often criticise people for not being generous.

Now ask yourself how those characteristics are relevant to you.

Example: In which areas of my life am I not generous? Am I truly generous with myself and others?

Now list the talents, attributes, skills and qualities that you notice and praise in others. Maybe their courage, their self-confidence, their charisma, their humour, their creativity, their talent. What's the quality you admire most? You can pick a specific person you look up to, or think more generally.

Ask yourself: Are there times you refuse to recognise these qualities in yourself?

Envision what it would look like if you embodied that quality right now. How it would change your work, relationships, life in general?

Example: I admire Victor for his honesty. How would my life change if I were more honest? What would change if I reclaimed this power? How would it feel to be able to voice my truest opinion when I am asked for it? How would it feel to be able to say no to an invitation when I don't feel like it? How would it feel to give an honest account of my experiences?

Then, act it out. David Richo writes, 'At first this means "acting as if" but soon we act with ease and even more of our hidden powers become accessible to us.'[12]

5

Letting Go of Our Identity

There is freedom within. The only freedom that truly exists –
freedom from the control we try to impose on ourselves.

•

Sometimes we need a push from life – to break down,
to come apart, to be disassembled, to un-become
and to un-create ourselves so that we can come
together in a new, bigger, bolder form, to move forward.

•

Our suffering does not just come from someone who is
doing something wrong to us, but mainly from the reason of
this situation, which we look for in ourselves.

We perceive the world through many different filters. As already explored, often what we think we are is nothing but a conglomerate of opinions we hold on ourselves at that moment, or opinions that we think others hold on us. Our brain has been programmed from early childhood by all the schematic behaviours, opinions and automatic reactions that surround us. For example, if someone grows up in a house with a father who shows no respect for women, they may well adopt the same behaviour and attitudes without question.

This process of socialisation teaches us not only to behave and react in a certain manner but also to judge according to certain patterns without considering the accuracy of our judgements; when we react to something, we usually 'label' it automatically.

Isn't that true? For example, if someone doesn't call us back right away we might think: How rude of them, or, It must mean they don't care.

Every one of us has been told from our childhood what is good and what is bad, what we should or shouldn't do and how we should or shouldn't be, what is right and what is wrong, whether by our parents, education, religion or a combination of these. We have unconsciously absorbed comments or criticism about ourselves from friends, family or teachers, and we have over time either come to believe these things about ourselves or rebelled against them, judging other people against these beliefs, in the same way as people have judged us.

For example, if your mum constantly told you how messy you were, did you start to believe it and actually become messy? Or did you become the very opposite: a super-tidy, uptight person, judging the messiness of others?

These views and opinions limit not only our perception of the world but also our questioning of who we are and what is right for us. If we operate on autopilot and respond to people's behaviours and situations in an automatic, programmed way, or if we judge what happens to us according to what we experienced a long time ago or what our parents experienced and have passed on to us, not only do we stop evolving as people but also we live this reality though many different filters that disconnect us from the possibility of seeing our life in the best possible way. How we look at things defines how we see ourselves. How we see ourselves defines how we feel. And how we feel defines the quality of our life. At every moment, at any time we have a choice. And the most important choice we have is in how we will look at our experiences and what meaning we will give them.

What Do You Believe You Shouldn't Be Doing?

I was once attending a lecture about sexuality at a conference. The speaker divided the room, maybe 500 people, into men on one side and women on the other.

Then the speaker said, 'Raise a hand who has ever lied about the number of sexual partners they've had.' Very few men raised their hands but, to my shock, about 90 per cent of the women did. Why have women become so afraid to speak their truth about their sexuality? I thought. The speaker asked another question: 'Who has ever faked an orgasm?' Again, about 90 per cent of the women raised a hand. This was the first time I'd truly realised how many women felt shame regarding their sexuality. I asked myself: *Is it truly more important for us to please a man rather than to please ourselves? Why would any woman fake an orgasm instead of guiding the man and showing him how to satisfy her? Why would any woman lie about the number of sexual partners she's had?* I realised that none of us wanted to be judged. We have been programmed to think that having many partners, and generally being sexually liberated, is wrong.

The lecture inspired me to give some more thought to the topic and I realised that my determination to not be 'too much' of a woman was created very early on. I remember when I was at secondary school, I had a big crush on a boy a year older than me. We started to spend some time together, hiking, biking and so on. Then one day, I heard some gossip that I was a 'slut' and that I was sleeping around. It devastated me. I wasn't sure who had spread it, but I cut contact with the boy as I was afraid that it might have been him. We had never even kissed. It broke my heart. From that day on I started

43

monitoring my behaviour so I could never be perceived as too easy or too sexually open. I was so afraid of judgement that I would verify every aspect of my behaviour to make sure that I was a 'good girl'. That I didn't show too much, that I wasn't too easy, that I didn't lose myself in my own pleasure. I can't even tell you how many urinary tract infections I have got after having sex because on an unconscious level I was feeling guilty or ashamed.

That experience of criticism at school meant I suppressed my sexuality, my sensuality and my femininity and blocked my body from fully accepting the physical pleasure for many years after, until I finally realised that I had been unconsciously judging not only myself for receiving physical pleasures but also other women for being 'too' liberated sexually.

After this realisation, for the first time I truly tasted what surrendering to physical pleasure could feel like without self-punishment, shame or guilt, without controlling and supervising myself and I freed myself from all sorts of limitations attached to it.

Perception Filters

We often prefer learning falsehoods from others to discovering truths on our own. We create filters through which we categorise, judge and schematise our reality and ourselves. Filters are like lenses we watch the world through. When we wear one, our vision is coloured by the glass shade and we don't even realise that the world could look very different without it. The glass shade represents here different beliefs, judgements and convictions, conscious and subconscious, which colour how we perceive everything we look at. The more filters we have around ourselves, often, the safer we feel. The more we think we know about others and ourselves, the more we feel that we have things under control. Our mind loves what's familiar and known, even if it is negative. It is frightened by the unknown. The familiar prison is better than unfamiliar freedom.

As we move through life we adopt different beliefs about ourselves. These often come from our environment. In one of her lectures at Mindvalley A-Fest in Jamaica, Nicole Brandfort talked about a 1,200-person academic study on people experiencing non-symbolic consciousness. This is a type of experience people have had, and spoken and written about, for millennia, often in religious and spiritual contexts, that is often referred to as enlightenment, persistent mystical states, non-duality, oneness, transcendental consciousness, and so forth. In this study, the researchers made quantitative and qualitative assessments to understand how participants were experiencing reality in the areas of cognition, emotion, perception and sense of self. They discovered that people from the same traditions living in different locations have less in common than people from different traditions living in the same location. For example, Buddhists from the same tradition living in different locations will have less in common than Buddhists, Catholics and atheists living in the same location. What does this mean? It means that where we live and who we hang out with has a much bigger impact on how we perceive our world than what we believe about the world. It is our surroundings that influence our perceptions the most, creating the filters that we see the world through. Therefore our parents or the people we grew up with, our siblings, our teachers and our group of friends will influence the most – although sometimes in a very subtle way – how we think. Much more than what we deliberately choose to believe about the world. Interesting, right? That's why it is so important to be aware of these influences that create the filters through which we perceive our reality, so we can learn to slowly strip them off.

Five Friends

In the words of motivational speaker Jim Rohn, 'You are the average of the five people you spend the most time with.'

The sum of the people you spend the most time with shapes who you are. They determine to which attitudes, behaviours, mentalities you are exposed. Eventually you start to take on and replicate certain thought processes, certain manners and conduct.

Think about who you spend your time with:

- How do the people you spend your time with perceive life? What is their attitude, lifestyle and perception of the world? What are their beliefs about life and themselves?
- Do you spend your time with people who inspire and motivate you or who take your energy?
- Do they participate in your growth or are they holding you back from it?
- What do you think those people think of you? Is it what you might think about yourself? Be honest with yourself.

I believe that we choose who we are in every moment. Every moment we have a chance to modify, adjust and create a new behaviour and a new attitude. And every moment we have a choice of how we will act and react. If we are surrounded by people who put us down in any way, it's very hard to initiate a change. Once we absorb limiting belief about life and ourselves, we adopt the filter that defines our perception and we re-create the same behaviours and circumstances, the walk, the same pathways and we keep attracting the same kind of people.

If we consider our opinion of ourselves to be 'truth', nothing on earth will persuade us that things are different. If a woman believes she is unattractive because her first partner told her so, even if a handsome man tells her she is beautiful she will not believe him. She will think he must be trying to fool or lie to her and will question his intentions. He is telling her his genuine opinion, yet she is not able to accept it – because then she would have to question her own way of thinking.

Dr Joe Dispenza, bestselling author and researcher, explains this in his book *Becoming Supernatural: How Common People Are Doing The Uncommon*:

The repetition of doing the same exact routine every day, thinking the same way, acting the same way, feeling the same way over and over again makes us go on autopilot. And if it is your environment and people in your life that are controlling your feelings then we could say that your Personal Reality is creating your Personality and you don't think, act or feel greater than your Personal Reality. The person becomes a victim to the circumstances in his/her life. In order for us to be greater in those conditions we need to be greater than our body and greater than our environment so it no longer controls our feelings and thoughts. So in order for you to change your Personal Reality you would have to change your Personality.[13]

Fascinating, isn't it?

But how do we change our personality; those old beliefs we have adapted for ourselves? People's personalities change through either repetition or, sometimes, emotional shock. In the journal from 1699 – 'Long lasting personality changes after the onset of dissociative amnesia', A. Staniloiu and H. J. Markowitsch write: Changes in personality dimensions occur after the onset of amnesia. These may involve affectivity, perception (e.g. impaired self face or face-emotion processing), cognition (e.g. social cognition) and behaviour (e.g. changing in eating, smoking, drinking or working habits).

This shows that if we remove the memory of our experiences we also remove the beliefs about ourselves associated with those experiences. Meaning, if we unattached from our past, we set ourselves free to create ourselves anew. Every experience in our life creates a thought, every repeated thought creates a belief, cultivated beliefs create mentality and persisted mentality creates our personality.

In order for us to keep adhering to our opinions our mind has to keep confirming them, over and over again. We need proof that what we think about ourselves is true. If we believe we are unpunctual (maybe because we've been told so by someone in our past), we will create that experience in our reality in order to 'prove' to ourselves that our belief is real.

But, as we've looked at already, we can't be absolutely sure that our thoughts about ourselves are always true, can we? These are just ideas created by past experiences or opinions of others, nothing else, and in order to change them, we have to let go of our identity. Doing so, we free ourselves to re-discover and re-create ourselves every single day.

We can choose new behaviours and create a new, more positive way of being until it becomes a new way of life. Our identity is nothing but a mental image of ourselves held in the mind. The fewer negatives we imagine, the fewer limits we create. The more positive opinion we hold about ourselves the more open we become to new possibilities. But I believe that the real sense of freedom comes from not being attached to either too-positive or too-negative opinions about ourselves and simply accepting whatever comes and shows up in us with an intention to experience ourselves with love and kindness every single day. When we don't assume that we know who we are, we can keep experiencing and discovering ourselves every day rather than trying to fit into an idea, often much smaller of what is truly possible for us to become. It is a beautiful process of revival, learning about oneself and about our own potential as well as falling in love with oneself and with life. It is a path towards freedom.

Self-Respect

We're often afraid of being ourselves because all the dark parts of our personality scare us. We run away from negative parts of ourselves, fearing rejection. We do not want to spoil the image we have created. We accept ourselves only when we are accepted by others (unfortunately, this does not work the other way round). We perpetuate a vision of ourselves and we do not want to destroy it. We become attached. We have to keep receiving evidence that this vision is true. That is why we feel so good among friends; we build upon their image of us. The more people show us love and respect, the better we feel.

But shouldn't it be the other way round? Surely it should be our respect for ourselves that compels the respect of others? Our self-love that should fascinate others? Unfortunately, we often build our happiness on the basis of someone else's attitude and opinion towards us instead. What happens if that attitude and opinion is not positive? What if we believe that other people perceive us badly? We feel down, rejected and not loveable. We feel that our world is falling apart. The positive opinions of others built our comfort, so when that vision shatters, there is nothing to build on and we hit rock bottom. We keep asking, *Am I so awful? What have I done? Why am I being rejected?* Then, we often blame ourselves by thinking, *It's my fault, I'm hopeless, I'm not good enough, I am not loveable, I am not interesting enough, I am too much* etc. We focus on our shortcomings. Instead of clear glasses we put on the dirty ones, through which we can't properly see who we truly are.

Self-judgement is the most self-destroying mechanism we can have. If we inform the universe that we are good for nothing, that people reject us, that people don't understand us, we attract more events of that kind. Each negative filter and every belief concerning our weaknesses will influence our reality, attracting events that back it up.

I believe we always have a choice and we can decide to believe the reality we desire.

It is good to remember that the image of ourselves we have in our own eyes and minds is nothing more than that – an image created upon everything we have ever seen, heard and experienced. If, out of the blue, we lost our memory, we would forget who we were yesterday and for the last twenty years of our life; we would lose our identity. We would have to create our personality anew. We would have to discover ourselves from the very beginning and new experiences would create an entirely different perception of ourselves than the one we once had. What if we didn't have to lose our memory in order to re-create ourselves? What if we could commit to discovering ourselves anew every single day? What if we could simply ask ourselves every morning when we wake up: Who do I wish to be today and how do I wish to be? Perhaps we are one question away from becoming who we always wanted to be. We can change absolutely anything and everything about ourselves internally if we truly desire it. Everything depends on us.

Taking Things Personally

The opinions of others may be only a projection, or they may contain useful knowledge to point us towards understanding our unconscious behaviours. In either case there is no need to be hurt by them.

We only take things personally when there is a seed of truth in what was said, or when they trigger a memory from the past. The memory activates an emotion and we then automatically assume a similar scenario to the one in the past and we activate a self-defensive reaction.

This situation has happened to me. I was in a restaurant with a friend and got up first to initiate leaving. My friend asked, 'Do you always lead like that?'

Someone else might have simply smiled and said, 'Sure, I love leading, but we can stay longer if you want.' But I reacted with a sarcastic comment: 'Well, someone has to take the lead.' Boom! Automatic fight response to an assumed attack, without a second of reflection. My friend didn't mean anything bad but I saw in his comment thousands of past criticisms of me being 'too strong', 'too masculine' or 'too intimidating' and it triggered me massively.

Things become personal because we make them personal. If there were ten people in the room, every single one of those people would react to this comment differently depending on their own experiences, beliefs, opinions and memories. If we didn't have any memories or feelings about an issue, we might feel curious about someone else's comment or behaviour but we would not get triggered. That's why every trigger is always a great source of information about what is going on inside you: what still has to be addressed, realised or seen. For me at the restaurant, the truth was that I was dictating, I wanted to lead and to control the situation; and I didn't want to see it in myself. Because I believed that 'too-masculine' women are not desirable I rejected this part of myself. I wanted to be more feminine, gentle and open. The true change however is impossible when we reject any part of ourselves, a good or bad one. Before we can choose who we would like to become, we need to fully own who we are here and now. It's the full acceptance of ourselves that reunites our rejected selves and opens us up for a change. Today, I know how to be and love both of these parts. I know when to use my leadership skills and when to soften and surrender to my feminine side. I have learned how to dance between two energies without any need to classify myself as either masculine or feminine. All of us have an entire spectrum of these same emotions and possibilities. Today, I don't have to choose to be one or another, I can be both and that is so much more empowering. Perhaps, the secret is to be all of it and to be nothing at all.

Taking Constructive Criticism

If someone offers us constructive feedback, it's wise to watch how we react to it before drawing any conclusions. We only can feel hurt by negative feedback when there is a seed of truth in it, we have a dissimilar image of ourselves and we want to be right about ourselves at all costs. When we don't want to see the full aspects of who we are and we are unable to accept our own imperfections, we often try to protect ourselves from others' feedback by attacking or rejecting them, but it only happens because we ourselves are feeling rejected. We feel judged and misunderstood. In reality, we experience these defensive or angry feelings because we do not accept and own all the parts of ourselves. The judgement of others can't harm us if we don't judge ourselves. If we behave wrongly, if we make a mistake, then our concern should be to improve the situation and act like the person we would like to be. Having someone in front of us who can see us, guide us and show us our blind spots is a true treasure.

Unfortunately, because of our not fully accepting all the parts of ourselves, we often react instead with shame, guilt or anger towards ourselves and create even more self-rejection rather than giving ourself permission to be a human and make mistakes. It is good to remember that no one is perfect. By giving ourselves permission to be imperfect, we give ourselves proof of unconditional self-love. Sometimes it is easier to know who we are if we contrast it with who we are not. After all – the stars shine brighter at night.

When we know who we are and we own all parts of ourselves, no negative feedback can harm us. We will either agree with someone's remark and be able to admit and recognise our imperfections, or we will internally know that the person blames us for their own flaws. We will feel that it's just a projection of the parts of themselves that they have rejected. In both cases we will feel secure and confident.

> Self-confidence doesn't come from gaining
> more knowledge, more wealth, more compliments
> and more personality, but from giving up
> the fear of not knowing, not having,
> not being seen and not being perfect.

Ourselves and Our Relationships

Our suffering does not just come from someone who is doing something wrong to us, but mainly from the reason for this situation, which we look for inside ourselves.

When we meet and understand ourselves, we will understand what is important, what we desire and who we want to be. Then we will no longer need to hold other people responsible for our happiness, self-acceptance and self-love. Our own opinion of ourselves will no longer depend on what others think of us. And our relationships will no longer be the key to our happiness but the way of expressing our happiness.

As long as we do not have the feeling of safety within, no marriage, home or family will guarantee it. The feeling of lack of safety will come up, in different forms, again and again. The same goes for lack of love, abundance and trust. These may manifest themselves in suspicion towards a partner, in the invention of non-existent problems, or in being obsessively jealous. In every case, we will push our partner away.

But if we can approach our partner without expectations, without the need for acceptance, there is no space for disappointment or suffering, for we are the radiant, happy version of ourselves. When we can accept ourselves for who we are, we can also accept others for who they are and we don't need them to behave in a certain way to fulfil our needs. We do not need the approval of others to love ourselves. And when we do love ourselves, regardless of external factors, the love and respect of others is inevitable.

Five Friends

Write on a piece of paper the names of the five people you speak with or hang out with the most, and ask yourself honestly for each one:

1. How do I feel about myself when I'm with this person? Write down the feelings that come to mind.
2. How do I think this person perceives me? Write this down. Is this how you choose to see yourself?
3. Is this person pushing me up or pulling me down? Write 'Up' or 'Down' next to every name.
4. Why am I friends with this person? What does this person offer me? How does this person contribute to my life?

Look at what you've written. Reflect on your answers. Ask yourself: Do I choose to stay in these relationships for the wrong reasons? What are those reasons? What do I believe I am getting out of these relationships? Who uplifts me and who pulls me down? Do my friends truly perceive me in the way I imagine? Perhaps I can ask them?

When we become upgraded versions of ourselves many people won't want to see our growth and our change. They prefer to see us through an old filter that doesn't support our growth. They stick to an idea of us from a long time ago – people simply like what is familiar. And some people don't see us at all, they just see in us a reflection of themselves that they either accept or reject. Choose to hang out only with people who see you for who you truly are. Surround yourself with people who are committed to witnessing your growth every day, who can be your mirror and who can love all aspects of you, because they can love all aspects of themselves. Don't let other people's criticisms influence who you choose to become every day.

6

Self-Creation

To know how to create you often need to
learn how to destroy first.

•

I would prefer to live in my dream of a better world
that might never come true, rather than trying
to fit into a vision much smaller then myself.

Achieving Our Desires

We all desire something. More wealth, more love, more security, more success, more joy or more inspiration.

Why? To **feel** more wealthy, more loved, more secure, more successful, more joyful or more inspired. Everything we desire is there for us to make us **feel** in a certain way.

We believe that in order for us to experience that feeling, some external conditions have to be fulfilled first.

'I will feel more inspired if there is more inspiration in my life.'

'I will feel more wealthy if I have more money.'

'I will feel more loved if I get married.'

We crave that specific external condition that we imagine will create the very feeling we are lacking. We wait for that condition to appear in our life in order to finally feel what we desire to feel so much.

But is it the reality that creates us? Or is it us who creates our reality? What do you think?

I believe that everything comes from us and is a reflection of us. Every feeling, every thought, every action is creating what our reality looks like and has an effect on what comes back to us. Have you ever noticed that we always attract **what we are**?

So ask yourself:
- Is it possible to attract wealthiness if you **feel** unwealthy?
- Is it possible to attract love if you **feel** unloved?
- Is it possible to attract success if you **feel** a failure?

If you wake up every day with a feeling of lack, you are going to experience it. And your reality will simply be a physical extension of **who** you are.

Now, is wearing expensive clothes, driving an expensive car or having two million pounds in your bank account the only things that can make you feel wealthy?

No. They are just by-products of your true wealth.

So would you then agree that, if I wake up every day with a feeling of wealthiness, I am not only gaining more chances to attract it into my life, but I am also going to find it easier to create?

Have you ever fallen in love and suddenly felt increased interest and attention from other people? It is not because you suddenly look more beautiful, it's because you are generating the information *'I am loveable'* instead of *'Nobody loves me'*.

All the feelings that you can think of are already **inside** you: those feelings you experience every day and those feelings you dream of experiencing.

Having all those feelings inside you already means that it is in your power to either change them or to activate them. It is not **having** that creates them, though, it is **doing** and **being**.

Becoming familiar with those feelings and discovering that you can access them in many different ways will change how you perceive yourself. And when you change the way you perceive yourself, your whole reality changes.

We Do Not Become Our Reality, Our Reality Becomes Us

Feelings are energy that emanates from the body. This energy attracts people and events of identical vibration. If I expect someone to give me love, I will attract a person with the same expectations. And everything around me is connected with what is within me. Therefore, I can either see myself as a victim of my own reality or I can interpret my reality as information about myself, about what is happening inside of me. And the things I ignore will come back intensified. Focusing on lack of love, or on suffering, will bring nothing but more suffering and more lack of love.

My reality does not result from what I do,
but from who I am.

Can you learn to look at yourself now as you would like to see yourself tomorrow, regardless of your reality? I often ask myself: *What kind of person must I become in order to achieve what I want? How must I dress, behave and speak? What must I believe? What kind of energy must I generate?* Everything starts in our mind. Let us give the world our favourite colours. Here and now. In our imagination. Then let's speak it out. I believe that the biggest influence we can have on our life is by what we think and speak, how we feel and act. Feel your future self, speak your future self, think as your future self and act as your future self.

Start now. Life will lead you to the place where you are meant to be. In fact life will lead you even further – to a place you haven't even imagined.

Sometimes it is good to leave some space for the unimagined things that life would like to offer.

Trusting In Life

Life knows best what is good for us and what we need. We should trust this. The more we try to control our space, the more we block what life is offering. If we have a very precise vision of our future, we limit the enormous possibilities of the universe. To some extent, our imagination can limit us, for we are not able to imagine things we do not know or to create a picture in our mind of anything we don't consider feasible. The universe, however, is limitless and does not function according to logical patterns. It can offer us far more than we can dream of.

It took me years of consideration to realise that everything that happens to us is predetermined because we are the architects of our own fortune. I understand now that one of these things does not eliminate the other: it is as if we had a picture to paint – life gives us the canvas and the paints but we decide what is in the picture. So, at the same time, everything is determined in advance and nothing is determined at all.

The world constantly wants to help us and push us forward – although we decide whether or not to make use of it. And everything comes down to one thing: discovering oneself. To put it differently: experiencing oneself; connecting with one's soul. We decide whether we go forwards or backwards. We are cast into the river but we decide whether we go with the flow or not. Trying to control things is senseless, for it denies the power of the universe. Control makes us too dominant, greedy for perfection, and eventually frustrated and hyper-critical. When you aspire to perfection you will never attain it, for perfection is here and now – assuming we can see it. If we can, we will feel satisfaction and fulfilment. Everything that surrounds us is for our own good. That does not mean though that we shouldn't develop, make plans, or change.

So, let us paint life with colours of our choice, yet when something unexpected happens, let's welcome it with open arms. Let's try not to control it. Let's accept. Let's surrender. Whatever happens, it always happens as a result of our process and it's there to make us grow. It might be the beginning of a change for the better.

Whatever we think, say and do creates an effect. Therefore we can say that we create in every moment of our life. Every action has a reaction, and so the more we act the more we create. When we act we send energy to the universe and begin to communicate with it. Then the universe is able to answer. Only, we must listen. We will be led to exactly the place we are intended to be, that will illustrate to us where we are at.

Start to paint the landscape of your life and try to express yourself in the things you have an affinity for. Create your internal universe, which will then express itself in your physical reality, and witness every single day the beauty of who you are, inside and outside of yourself.

61

Live your life as if every day was special, because every day teaches you a little bit more about who you truly are. Can you see it?

I-FEEL-ME

On a piece of paper write how you would like to FEEL about yourself.

What generates those feelings inside you? What action can you take in order to feel those feelings about yourself today?

For example: I would like to feel healthy. I feel healthy when I go for walks outside, when I exercise for at least ten minutes per day, when I eat healthy food. What can I do today to feel healthy? Today I can go for a walk outside.

Or: I would like to feel rich. I feel rich when I go out to a nice restaurant, when I treat myself with a nice gift, when I am generous with my friends, when I host dinner parties. What can I do today to feel wealthy? I can treat myself with a massage.

Invite this feeling into your life today.

7

Emotional Freedom

The more you try to escape what is inside you,
the more trapped you feel, wherever you go.

•

There are two ways of living. Inside your mind or outside
of it. Only one of them can ever make you feel alive.

•

Our well-being is entirely based on our perception
of every situation we choose to adopt.

The Idea of Freedom

Every day of our life brings a range of emotions. We feel both
positive heart-warming emotions and those negative ones that
bring us down. The first ones let us enjoy life, enhance our
potential and positively influence our relations with others.
The negative ones, however, cause limitations and deprive us
of strength.

Once upon a time, I used to let my feelings hop and run freely.
I might have fallen but the wounds used to heal fast. My feelings
were free.

But then I put them on a leash, tried to control them. For a
while I didn't even let them run in the wrong direction. However, that self-made leash, tangled by fear and loneliness, was
quite resistant. It sometimes got knotted and twisted and
became difficult to untangle.

In my experience, we often tie our feelings up, numb the sensations in our body without letting them speak up or trying to understand them. The more we suppress our emotions, the more restricted we feel. We will then look for that sense of freedom everywhere else instead.

Freedom represents different things for different people – financial independence, a nomadic lifestyle, freedom to express our ideas without censure, the ability to travel and live anywhere we choose, the choice to do whatever we want to do, whether that is polyamory or the life of a single person.

What does it mean to you?

But if we consider or hope that fulfilling these conditions, which all live outside of ourselves, will make us feel differently inside, they have control over us, right? We are letting them control how we feel.

Is it possible to feel free even if none of these conditions are achieved?

And is it possible to have achieved all of these conditions and still not feel free?

I have realised that it is not so much the power we give to external things that creates this constant chase for freedom, love or happiness, but more the disempowerment we give to ourselves as we chase it. We try to become free from what we feel and from that which we fear the most. We may think that is poverty, lack of a home, not having a job, not being in a relationship or not having love. But could it be possible that what we fear most is actually ourselves? Our own shadows, our own feelings and emotions, our own judgement, our shame or guilt, our anger or sadness? Our own disappointment about ourselves? Our pain?

So the biggest restriction we create is the one we place on ourselves.

By controlling the outside world, all we truly desire is to control how we feel. But if we try controlling something it means something controls us.

What is it that you fear the most?

It is not the lack of money that frightens us but our interpretation of it. It is not marriage itself that scares us but our judgement or definition of it. It is not the lack of a house that creates our insecurity but our perception of it.

What Is Freedom?

Freedom for me is the end of trying to escape from one's own emotions and attempting to change them. It is the acceptance that I and only I am responsible for what I feel. It is an understanding that I have a choice.

> The only freedom that
> truly exists is freedom from the control
> we try to impose on ourselves.

So if you do have a desire to experience freedom in any way and you are not feeling it within yourself, it means you are controlling yourself.

Can you answer truly: How much do you control yourself?

How many things do you try to impose on yourself and others? Do you like things to be done 'your way'? Do you need to plan and know things in advance? How much are you afraid of 'letting go'? How much are you afraid of the unknown? How much are you avoiding what you truly feel?

There is no place you can run to or anything you can get that will let you escape from confronting yourself. We try to numb ourselves with alcohol, drugs, games, television, work – anything in order to not feel something or to feel something different. What kind of freedom is that really?

- The more you try to control how you feel, the less free you really are.
- The more you let the external world dictate your state of being, the more you limit yourself.
- The more you try to escape what is inside you, the more trapped you feel, wherever you go.

Freedom means to stop escaping. It means to stop controlling. It is letting go.

One day I realised that I had been hiding from fear my entire life. Not escaping anything specific, but trying to escape fear itself. I was so afraid of feeling afraid that I would do anything to not feel it.

I realised that real freedom wasn't liberation from fear but liberation from constantly running away from it.

The more I tried to suppress my feelings and emotions, the more I was trying to control myself and the world around me.

In this way I was never really experiencing myself or others but only my own controlled perception of them. And the only way to really experience oneself is to set the self free.

Types of Emotions

In this chapter I would like to focus on our emotions and understanding them better. If we understand better what we fear the most, we might realise that it is not that scary at all.

Emotions and feelings don't have to be our enemy; they can become our friend, who will guide us through life. For many years I thought I was feeling, but I wasn't feeling at all. My body was completely numb. I accumulated so many negative emotions inside that I would do anything to not feel them. But if we have too many unexpressed emotions inside our body they can take control of our life without us realising it. Let me explain how and why.

I've spent years studying human feelings and have divided them into three groups. The first group is natural feelings, the ones coming from our higher Self, which are nothing but information that we experience through brief feelings within the body, caused by particular situations, events or persons. They can also be called our intuition.

The second group consists of unnatural feelings resulting from thoughts, which originate from the conscious or subconscious mind.

The third group, the most difficult to discover, are recorded feelings.

Natural Feelings

The feelings that appear before the process of thinking are always natural. They are often incomprehensible, difficult to control, and unexpected. We should not restrain these feelings. After all, when the magma undergoes compression, the volcano erupts.

We are taught not to show feelings; or, for various reasons, we decide not to do so. Yet, our feelings are a gift. They are designed to help us go through life. They are our guidelines. André Charbonnier says in his book *It Could Have Been Worse* that when we are not able to decipher an emotion, we start to identify with it.[14] We become it. We think that we are sad, as a person, rather than that 'we feel sadness', which is a reaction to or an outcome of a particular situation. We will be stuck in that negative emotion as long as we do not respond properly to it. Each emotion is a message intended for you. It is the purest expression of our deepest truth and must be deciphered and transformed. In other words, it tells us the truth about a particular situation.

The message is released by our endocrine glands, our hormones. We can also call it the intuition of our body. Have you ever felt an anxious cramp in your stomach when someone invited you to do something? That was probably your body communicating with you and warning you about getting involved. How many times have you ignored this feeling? Those feeling are not supposed to last longer than a few seconds; they are supposed to express the message and leave our body. But if we ignore them, they will remain until we accept something, change it or end it. Suppressed feelings cause and worsen dysfunctional reactions because we are not in alignment with ourselves.

Elisabeth Kübler-Ross wrote about five natural feelings: anger, grief, envy, fear and love.[15] Anger makes a tool that enables us to refuse. We do not have to offend others; anger does not have to hurt people. But when it is suppressed, it can change into a disease or fury (Neale Donald Walsch writes about this in his book *Conversations With God*[16]), which is a very unnatural feeling. When we watch children expressing their anger we can see them screaming, jumping, shaking their fists, running around or crying. They are not hurting anyone around them but just letting their emotions out. When we experience a stressful situation our body starts shaking or sweating in order to let the negative energy out. Suppressing our emotions only increases them. Suppressed grief can become depression, envy can change into jealousy, and fear into panic. Strangled love can become possessiveness. That is why we should never suppress our emotions.

When we live our truth, we naturally feel positive emotions. And the mother of positive emotions is love.

Negative emotions and positive results

The further we move away from our truth, the more negative emotions are released. Fear is their father. Positive emotions tell us that something is good for us and we should continue. Negative ones inform us about unfavourable situations and protect us from getting into them.

These emotions can't be deceived or changed at will. However, they can be suppressed and accumulated. Accumulated emotions are called stress.

Stress must be released; holding it within is not healthy for our mind and body. In order to deal with stress, our mind invented a system for 'evacuation,' i.e. complaining. It hardly ever brings us a solution to the problem, yet we feel relief for a moment. Complaining, however, creates a lot of negative energy around us by focusing on the problem and, consequently, attracts more and similar energy and problems. It is a vicious circle and I'll speak about this more in later chapters. Unfortunately, complaining is the most popular form of exteriorising bad emotions. We then have to deal with the phenomenon of identifying with those emotions. We must understand that we do not need to control our emotions, but that it is crucial that we hear and understand what these particular emotions want to tell us. Then we can release them and let them circulate freely.

Once I was invited to a friend's wedding party. We live very far apart, but on this occasion I was due to be on a business trip and staying closer by. I was excited about the prospect of going, and spending time with her; yet at the same time I felt strange discomfort within – like someone was squeezing my stomach. I couldn't understand where this feeling was coming from. It would be fantastic to participate in such a joyful event. Yet the feeling was growing. I couldn't sleep. I was stressed. I felt repelled by the idea of going. Eventually, I decided to trust my intuition, and regretfully turned down the invitation.

As it turned out, the day before the wedding, my plans suddenly changed and I was required to attend a conference in a different area. Neale Donald Walsch himself was there. We met and we've been friends ever since.

That time turned out to be one of the most important periods in my life. I encountered many new facets of myself, I deepened my knowledge, and I managed to help many people solve their dilemmas. My greatest accomplishment at this time, however, was that I started to trust my intuition implicitly. I know now that it leads us to precisely the place we are meant to be and where we are really needed the most.

Unnatural Feelings

Unnatural feelings are born out of the process of thinking. They can be created by conscious or unconscious thoughts. We can somewhat easily recognise the ones that originate from conscious thoughts, but it's more difficult to recognise unnatural feelings when they arrive out of our subconscious. Usually, we do not know where they come from. Therefore, they require diligent study. Feelings created by the subconscious mind are often connected with past events.

The character of subconscious thoughts

Let us imagine the following situation: We were in a relationship with someone from a different country to ourselves and he hurt us badly when the relationship ended. One day, we're at a party and meet someone else from the same country. We feel aversion and convulsions in the stomach when we listen to that person speaking and their accent that reminds us of the person who hurt us. Is it really our intuition that is telling us to beware of that guy? Or is it rather the association with the past trauma that has created this programme, a programme designed to protect us from similar situations?

Every trauma creates in our brain a kind of imprint, which later on can sabotage our feelings and reactions through subconscious beliefs we collect about the world. The other person or a situation is never the cause of any emotion but rather a trigger that points at the subconscious belief creating the emotional reaction. Even with the same situation, two or more people can never react the same, because every person holds different memories, traumas or associations, which will create very individual reactions. As mentioned before, every reaction is activated by association with a bad memory from the past. For instance, if our partner had a bad day and is very cold with us, and we have past experiences where coldness was a signal for a lack of love and interest or was a form of a punishment for bad behaviour, we will start to panic. We are holding on to a belief that coldness means rejection or that we have done something wrong. We take the coldness personally and make it all about us because to us, it is personal. Our mind creates a story: He doesn't love me any more, it's going to be over, I am going to suffer again. What have I done wrong? The story activates fear. And fear activates an emotional reaction. If we didn't have any bad memories associated with coldness and a lack of affection, we would simply give the person some space and focus on something else. We would be confident enough to not take it personally and would simply wait until it passes.

71

To change our subconscious thoughts we need to first realise what they are and where they come from. I'll discuss this more in the coming chapters.

The character of conscious thoughts

Consciously created feelings, however, are often linked with the present or the future. They are the results of our thoughts about particular situations or our vision of that situation in the future. According to Russian philosopher Peter Ouspensky, there are four causes of negative emotions:

- justification
- identification
- inward considering
- blame[17]

Negative emotions depend on our perception of the situation here and now, on the assumptions we make.

Once I was at a four-day music festival in Belgium. A stranger approached me and asked if he could use my mobile to contact his girlfriend. His battery had died the day before and finding electricity was difficult. When he called his girlfriend on my phone, he explained to her why he'd been unable to text her back and assured her of his feelings. She responded that she loved him, and apologised for all the bad things she had written to him when she was unable to contact him and hadn't heard from him.

So, one little thought can grow to an enormous size. It can create huge, unnatural emotions and cause us to make hasty decisions with very real consequences that we might regret later. Yet these emotions are produced simply by our imagination.

David Berceli, in his book *A Man Made of Clay: Help Me to Heal Myself,* describes what happened when refugees in Ethiopia could not contact their families due to armed combat in the region.[18] Their relatives had no idea if their kin were still alive, and their heads were full of nightmarish images about what might have happened. The experience of those involved in the combat was real and physical; the experience of their relatives was based on illusion, cut off from the feelings in the body. When the combat ended, those who survived it were in much better emotional shape than those who had only imagined what might have happened to their families. Berceli observed that the victims of trauma had a better attitude to life than those who had imagined many different unfortunate events and were full of resentment, fear and spite.

Berceli's observations of this situation show that imagining negative scenarios is much more damaging to our psyche than actually living the negative scenario and results in much more negative perceptions of life in general. Our thoughts are often much worse enemies than our actual enemies. Put another way, the perception of our reality is more important than the reality itself. We can have everything in the world, but if we are not able to see our life as a gift we will never be happy.

Reprogramming our thoughts

In the same way that our thoughts can create some negative, destructive scenarios, they can also be the source of positive feelings. For example, if we receive an unexpected message from someone we love, a present, or a surprise, we can become suddenly very joyful. That's because at that very moment, we change our view of the situation and of ourselves. We feel appreciated and seen. It is not the situation per se that makes us happy but our own interpretation of this situation and what we think about it. We can't stop the thoughts in our mind but, knowing that the thoughts constantly influence how we feel, we can choose the character of them. If we are irritated by our neighbour's loud music, we have to either leave our flat, ask them to turn it down, or just accept it, otherwise we will not be able to concentrate and simple irritation may morph into anger. Our well-being is entirely based on our perception of every situation we choose to adopt and the choice we make. We have the power to see life the way we choose to see it, no matter what reality we live in or what the truth is about our situation. If we adopt a positive vision of ourselves, focus on what we choose to see and abandon pessimistic thoughts or fears that trap us, our life will change for the better. If we learn not to judge, and assume that everything happens for our good, we will get rid of fear and suffering and we will start to trust.

In contrast to natural feelings, we can control our unnatural feelings by learning to control our thoughts. We cannot stop thinking, but we can choose our thoughts more carefully. Every single thought creates emotion; so let's make these thoughts positive and optimistic. Then our mood and the reality around us will align according to it.

Thoughts and emotions we do not feed fade. We are bombarded with an unlimited number of thoughts, but consciousness can only deal with one thing at a time. It can't think and feel at the same time and it can't think about both negative and positive scenarios at once. So if we change a negative thought to a positive one, we will have only that positive thought. Changing our thoughts and programming our mind to think positively is a matter of training, awareness, commitment – but mostly a choice. We always have the choice in what we think about any situation. It is a matter of perspective, of our attitude, of our perception. If our partner tells us he/she is going to spend an evening with friends, we can take it personally and feel left alone, rejected. Or we can see it as a great opportunity to have some time for ourselves. Read, watch a movie, speak to a few friends and so on. The more insecure we are, the more negatively we will judge the situation. The more bad memories we have associated with this kind of behaviour, the more we will reinforce our insecurity by choosing to see it as negative. If we go on assuming that everything that happens is perfectly designed for our growth and we are always in the exact right place where we are supposed to be because it reflects exactly where we are at internally, then we will see every situation as an opportunity to evolve. Are you going to see the half of the glass that is empty or the half of the glass that is full? The choice is yours.

Ego

When we are born our mind is ready to be filled with information, like the hard disk of a computer. Our personality develops according to information recorded on the 'disk' of our experiences. Our character, our opinions, our taste are the result of how the files on the disk have been organised. That net of connections creates our personality and the voice of our ego. It is a result of billions of thoughts. Yet, these are only thoughts. As we have already seen, our life is like a canvas on which we can choose what to paint.

The ego is our engine. It destroys the white areas on the canvas so the soul can express itself. Therefore, ego destroys so that the soul can create. For that reason ego is necessary. If not for the ego, we would think we are what we can see. There wouldn't be any separation. And to discover oneness we need to understand the separation first.

75

If not for the ego we would not have the desire to help others, because others would not exist. We would not have any desire, period. The ego is the fuel, it is the motivation, it is the drive. The motivator to destroy the ego gives you the ego itself. So, the ego has its very important function. It is designed, however, not to take control over us but to fuel the creation of our reality. It must be our servant, not our master; the ship, not the captain.

Recorded Feelings

The third kind of feelings are ones we've either inherited or suppressed in our body. They are written down as energy. We can see them as karmic feelings recorded in the memory of our soul from previous incarnations; our ancestors' heritage, written in our genes; and/or created by unexpressed early traumatic life experiences. In all cases, they influence our physical body as well as our mood and the vibration of our aura, which others can sense.

Emotions are energy that can be kept and trapped in our body. This theory is connected to organ transplants; some transplant patients claim they are able to feel the emotions and moods of their donors. And there is evidence that even emotions we absorb through food (for example, meat) influence the way we feel, for the tissues 'accumulate' emotions and memories.

This can be connected with the fact that fasting has been widely used since early in human history, in civilisations including those of the ancient Egyptians, Greeks, Babylonians, the Native Americans of Mexico and the Incas of Peru (these last who observed fasting as a form of penance to their gods). And fasting is still employed now, in modern times. The three major world religions advise fasting at certain times – in Judaism during

Yom Kippur, in Christianity during the Lent period, and in Islam during the festival of Ramadan. Other major religions, such as Buddhism and Hinduism, also employ and highly recommend this practice. Fasting is believed to be the best method of communicating with the divine – in purifying the body, it is believed, we also purify the mind.

We create blocked energies in our body when we refrain from expressing our emotions. Suppressed emotions connected with stress can accumulate in different places in the body and can influence the mood of an individual, as well as the anatomy of that person, causing problems and illness.

The more energy accumulates through unexpressed emotion, the more negative energy imprints into our body and the bigger the impact it has on our emotional state and how we are perceived by other people, but also on how other people perceive us. We perpetually emanate the energy we have within. We may have good intentions, yet if we have unexpressed accumulated emotions, the signal we send into the world around us will be the opposite. I believe very strongly that recorded emotions, never released and instead imprisoned within, can not only influence our mental well-being but can also be the source of many physical health issues, created by our subconscious to remove the trapped energy from our body.

The intention of our subconscious

The basic function of our subconscious is to save and preserve our life. It always wants the best for us – but sometimes it doesn't work out that way. When we are filled with energetic blocks made up of accumulated negative energy, the subconscious will try, with all its might, to purify us. Traumas, imprisoned emotions

77

and unprocessed life experiences are all stored in the cells of our body as negative energy and can be the source of various dysfunctions.

Also, the release of traumatic memories hidden in our subconscious mind can cause stress. The subconscious does not see the difference between an emotional reaction to real events and the same reaction caused by just thoughts. Whenever an emotion or experience that was originally a real event is re-triggered by thoughts, our body reacts as if the same event is happening again in reality and is retraumatised. Within our body it is the same; it's as if this traumatic situation from our past was actually happening over and over again.

If we haven't processed an event from the past, then, the negative emotions from that event will be locked in our body and will attract similar situations until we release it. We will build mental blocks and our energy will stagnate. According to Dr Joe Dispenza, the scientific facts prove that the chemistry of stress disturbs our genes and makes them ineffective, leading to various afflictions. Thus, our thoughts can harm us. Thoughts generate feelings and then vibrations come. Each feeling represents a different kind of vibration. Vibrations create our reality by attracting or pushing away certain things, people and events. Therefore, when we change the vibration in our body, we may change the whole reality around us.

With recorded feelings our mind very often can't recognise where the negative emotions come from and tries to externalise them. It tries to find a situation or a person to blame or make responsible for how we feel, so it can 'fix' things by changing the situation or the surroundings. However, we will just attract the same situation again, because the internal issue is still the same. That's why it is very important to know that before we re-create our world we need to re-create ourselves and let the world simply reflect our change.

Liberation

Unfortunately, many people define themselves by past experiences and live and breathe past emotions. Those feelings are nothing more than a record of the past and only when we start to release it and change the vibration of our body can we start creating a new self.

If we keep the same emotional reaction in our body for some time, it becomes our mood. If we keep it for weeks, it becomes our temperament. After years it will form our personality. Therefore, if we want to change a particular character trait (aggression, possessiveness, jealousy etc.), we must examine the emotion that is the source of that trait. If we haven't processed an event from the past, the negative energy from that event gets locked in our body and will not only change our character but it will also attract similar situations until we release it. It will keep coming up as a pattern. We will keep 'retraumatising' ourselves, create the same emotional dynamics and build mental and physical blocks. But one day, month, or year shouldn't define the rest of our life.

In order to connect with something new, we have to disconnect from the things that used to hold us down. Emotions recorded deep within are more difficult to identify, because we didn't want to express them so we don't really recognise them. We rejected them, pushed them away and numbed ourself to not feel them. But if we limit our sensations of the pain, we automatically limit our access to joy. Anger and sorrow were given to us with life, as well as love and happiness. Therefore, they shouldn't be perceived as wrong; they are just a part of a whole experience of being a human. They have their function. The point is not to avoid anger, for example, but rather to discover how to purify yourself through anger. Crying, too, brings relief and purification. In every tear born of grief there is a seed of all the suffering we have ever experienced. There are hundreds of memories in each tear. That's why it is so important to cry. We are purified not only of the bad energy we have just created but also of all the bad energy we have collected over our entire life. Crying brings balance and peace of mind. It leads to physical and spiritual relief. Every emotion has its own function. Anger allows us to recognise peace, sadness allows us to recognise the joy.

My story

I had explored many techniques, including meditation, over a long time to help with the heavy weight I felt in my heart and the sense of a great pain from my past. It was still present, though. Talking to a friend about it, he commented, 'You may have disconnected from everything that caused you pain, but that does not mean that the pain has been released.'

I thought about this. Was it possible that there was trauma in my childhood so big that I had displaced the memory of it and also any related feelings? And was it possible that those unexpressed feelings were recorded in my body and had been influencing my life ever since?

The body holds enormous deposits of memory. I could feel there was an inner block I had to get rid of. I understood that the only way to do so was opening myself and releasing the unexpressed emotions.

But how does one do that? In order to release emotions, you must recognise them and let them speak.

My friend helped by sitting next to me and asking questions. I had never told my story before, for I didn't want to be judged, rejected, criticised. I didn't want to be known. I felt guilty whenever I admitted even the slightest weakness. Yet, the emotions suppressed in my childhood begged to be set free. It was not enough just to say them out loud; they had to be experienced once more. Now I would tell my friend my story.

As I mentioned before, I was rejected by my brother when I was little. I am guessing he felt rejected by our parents when I was born and he blamed me for it. Of course our parents loved us equally, yet as I was a girl, they were much more tough and strict with him. They still are. I can see now that it wasn't easy for him and his anger towards our father was projected on to me. We fought constantly, expressing hate for one another. The rage grew between us. He tried everything to make me feel miserable, unwanted, unloved. I tried everything to push him away, isolate myself from him or to hide from him. This relationship resulted in many scars, both physical and psychological, for both of us. I never experienced love from him. Later on, when I moved out of my parents' home at the age of sixteen, he and I cut contact with each other. Most of my friends didn't even know I had a brother. I would only see him when I would visit my parents but even then the brief exchange of words we would have, you could not even call politeness. Many times I tried to rebuild our relationship but I just didn't know how.

When I was around ten years old, I had a problem with my heart. One day at school, playing basketball, I started running towards the goal and suddenly everything went black. My heart started to beat at around 250 beats per second. I collapsed on the court. Later, I found out that if my heart rate hadn't slowed back down, as it did, within a few minutes, I would have died.

For years afterwards, the same thing would happen to me at least twice per week. I learned to shorten and manage the process by holding my breath or vomiting, which would slow down my heart rate. Eight years later, I was finally operated on for supraventricular tachycardia. I remember lying on the operating table with all the electrodes in my body, half unconscious, and the doctors had to wake me back up so I could sign a high-risk-procedure agreement. Interestingly, later in my life, my beloved dog suffered from exactly the same disease and died eleven years later.

But that was not my only illness. At the age of sixteen, I began to experience the first symptoms of what turned out to be a very rare bladder disease. I was in such extreme pain, but the doctors weren't able to diagnose the illness that was putting me in the hospital on a monthly basis. I heard from them over and over , 'We've tested everything, and the results all come back negative. The pain must be only in your mind.' Since I wasn't sure what to believe, I decided to save my money and visit a psychiatrist to see if he could find what was wrong with me. To my agitation, he told me, 'No, everything is fine, but I can still prescribe you some medication…'

I didn't know what to do. I felt completely helpless. This disease had cost me a normal life, normal relationships. So when I was nineteen, I decided to go to India.

Why India? Well, I was so sure that I would find a healer there who would miraculously cure me. I had read so much about all these mystical people living there, and I saw it as my chance for a miracle.

After three weeks in India, I arrived in the village of Sai Baba, one of the most famous healers back then. I immediately fell extremely sick with food poisoning. I thought it would get better after a couple of days but it didn't. After a week in a hospital, where the doctors tried all medications and nothing would work to stop my poisoning symptoms, I was transported by plane to the best hospital in New Delhi because there was a risk that, again, I might die. I remember my parents calling me, but I had no capability to speak. No capability to reassure my parents. No ability to even hold a phone in my hand. I honestly thought that was my end. But the doctors managed to find and destroy the rare bacteria that had been causing the symptoms and slowly life returned to my body. As soon as I was able to walk, I booked my flight back to Europe.

This episode caused me to have my first panic attacks. This was when I stopped believing in magic for the first time. I was afraid to travel; for a while I was even afraid of leaving my house. I continued living my life, taking a huge amount of painkillers and antibiotics, trying to ignore all the symptoms. I stopped showing people how much I was suffering. I stopped dreaming. Because, you know, when you are sick you have only one dream and that is to be cured.

But a few years later, I saw a light at the end of the tunnel. I was studying in Paris, and a great friend of mine, who is a doctor, was finally able to diagnose my bladder disease. She connected me with the best specialists in France. It felt like a sucker punch when they finally told me that there was no cure for it – interstitial cystitis – as the causes had not yet been fully studied.

I had hyper-distension of the bladder and was put on medication, along with daily painkillers.

The only thing that had changed was the fact that this time I knew for sure I wasn't crazy or imagining my pain. I still didn't know what to do. I felt completely helpless. By this time this disease had destroyed my normal life and relationships.

The illness and my past experiences made me feel less then other people. Damaged. I hadn't believed that I could be loved for who I am, so I believed I had to earn love. I also believed I had to earn the right to live. I wanted to be perfect, but I considered myself hopeless. I blamed myself for everything.

I told this story to my friend without any discomfort, as if I were reading a book. He marvelled at my ability to control my emotions. At one point, I said, 'I became really good at punishing myself for every symptom of imperfection.'

'That's it!' he exclaimed. 'That's your mantra! You had to be the best, even at punishing yourself. After years of being injured, you started to punish yourself, for it was something you learned from that painful experience. You loved people who punished you, so you started to believe you must do the same to yourself. You wanted other children to love you, yet you did not believe they could love you as you are. Trying to get their acceptance and being afraid of rejection you attracted exactly what you were afraid of. Your perfectionism became a tool for you to punish yourself. The disease you had when you met your first partner was your rebuke for love. You could not be loved, for you believed you did not deserve it.'

Then something burst inside me and I cried like a little girl. After years of unsuccessfully searching for the causes of my diseases, I finally understood they were rooted in my childhood. All tracks headed there. When I left home at the age of sixteen, I could not find a place to stay or a place to stop. For the next sixteen years, I lived in twenty-two different places all over the world. I kept travelling. I could not make a home, for home

84

meant danger and insecurity. My subconscious rejected all that. I could not build a relationship, for I felt subconsciously that love hurt and I was not loveable; I would either push it away or run away from it just like I did with my brother. Everything seemed to end with rejection – I was attracting exactly what I feared most. I started to tell myself, 'That's just what it's like with me. People just disappear from my life. How anybody could love me, if even my own brother rejected me?'

I believed nobody could love me for what I am, so I started to make an effort to become 'somebody'. I believed that unveiling who I really was could only result in rejection, so I started to put on various masks and armours so nobody could discover my true nature.

After I had this experience with my friend's help, something finally started to change. For a week, I woke up every day drenched in sweat. I experienced emotional fluctuations, heavy feelings that once brought into daylight were eventually ready to leave. It was an emotional detox.

What did these experiences bring and why I am writing about them? I believe that every bad experience leads towards something. The day that I decided to remove my mask, I started a wonderful relationship with myself. I became the most important person to myself. I 'married' myself, I forgave myself, I became open to myself. I promised that I would be true to myself and celebrate myself every day. I stopped doing and started being – being the best version of myself.

It is possible to remove accumulated and transmitted emotions from the body to speak, to be expressed, if these emotions are to be released. This is the only process that can possibly lead to absolute freedom, but it's not an easy one.

Eternity

Once I thought that everything ends. Now I know that everything undergoes perpetual transfiguration and is recorded in the abyss of eternity. Feelings that we experience for a while are eternal. Each emotion creates energy that is sent into the abyss of space. What we feel is always true, yet only in that particular moment. It means that a moment later we can feel something entirely different. Nothing is set in stone. Feelings constantly change. One day we think that somebody is the love of our life, and the next day we want to break up. It does not mean that what we had felt was not true, just that our thoughts, and then feelings, changed. It's actually quite natural. Life is a permanent evolution, change, transformation.

As we have seen, emotions will always be present. It's impossible to banish them. And we need both sides of emotion, good and bad; we know what joy is, for we know sorrow. We recognise light, for we have experienced darkness.

The feeling, whatever it is, might be eternal if we choose to stay plugged in to it. By staying plugged in to love itself, for example, you become love.

Love for ourselves is the most precious skill we can master. Self-love, which resides in all of us, is an absolutely necessary factor in the process of healing body and mind. Only by loving everything that you are and everything that you feel can you heal, liberate and realign yourself. By connecting with our heart, we start living in alignment with ourselves. We experience the natural state of love and happiness.

Let's allow the heart to guide us. It knows better. It knows what is good for us. Let's recognise what we carry inside, accept it and liberate it. Imagine that your body is like a glass full of trapped emotions. Any new emotion is mixed with everything you have accumulated over the years that you are not yet able to feel freely. Empty your glass, decide to consciously purify your body and mind of the baggage of old trapped emotions, false beliefs and negative thoughts. If you keep that baggage of bad experiences from the past, it will determine your emotions and, consequently, your reality. Your emotions will not be guiding you by draining you. In order to get through the process of purification, one must understand and accept the need to do it.

Belief Re-Creation

1. Write on a sheet of paper the things you fear the most. Describe your deepest fears. The fears that were born years ago. Write without restraint, without shame. Downplay nothing, even if you now consider them meaningless. Don't judge. Simply let it flow.

2. On another sheet of paper, change every sentence you have written about your fears into a positive statement/ affirmation, e.g. if you wrote 'I am afraid of people not trusting my words' you would change it to 'People trust and are inspired by my words. I trust and love myself.' Write down next to every statement a number from 1 to 4.
    1   I don't believe it at all.
    2   I believe it a little bit.
    3   I mostly believe it.
    4   I completely believe it.

3.   Now think of and write down at least three proofs that your statement is true, e.g. for 'People trust and are inspired by my words' you might write:
-   I got a nice message of appreciation for my social media post.
-   A friend thanked me for supporting her with my words.
-   I have been asked to give an interview based on the wisdom I share.

It might be a long process but it is worth it. Dealing with your subconscious beliefs is sometimes like going to court. If you can prove that your fear is 'irrational' it won't hold any power over you any more. After a week, try to rate yourself once again. Has your belief changed? What proofs in your external reality have you noticed after changing your belief?

Dance

For the next ten mornings, turn on your favourite music and dance as if there were no tomorrow. You have moved your mind; now it's time for you to move your body. Don't judge yourself. Don't look around. Just dance and enjoy the freedom. It will surprise you how wonderful you will feel.

I Love You For...

Write down on a sheet of paper, 'I love you for...' and leave a space after 'for'. Stick it to the mirror in your bathroom. Every morning and evening when you look at it finish the sentence. Say it out loud: 'I love you for...' Find at least three things that you love yourself for every single day.

It takes twenty-one days to reprogramme the mind. Stay committed!

8

How to Be Happy

You don't have to be good at anything in order to be happy.
When you are happy, no matter what you do it is done right,
because it's done from the heart.

•

Being happy is not getting what we want
but wanting what we get.

States of Happiness

How can we define happiness? It's a feeling of acceptance, joy and fulfilment combined.

It is a result of right thinking and right attitude towards the world and towards oneself. We can make ourselves feel exhilarated in just a moment by changing our attitude. Rather than crossing the continents searching for happiness, trying to buy happiness or expecting that happiness will come from another person, we'd be better off changing our perception of what happiness is. Why do we think happiness depends on external factors?

If you tell yourself that you will be happy when a particular condition is fulfilled, you may prevent yourself from experiencing it any sooner than that. And because you assume your happiness is conditional, every time you do make a dream come true, your happiness will last only a short while. You will keep searching for another condition, another thing, that might fill the void for a while.

In this consumer society, we have nice houses, fancy cars, kids at great schools... but even with all of this, we still find ourselves asking: Is this it? It feels like something is still missing, so we begin looking for more feelings and experiences to fulfil us. We want to change our current state. It is a paradox, but elevated states bring us nowhere else than straight back to the present moment. We escape the present to get ourselves back to the present.

Interesting, right?

What is an Ecstatic State?

All of the ecstatic states – including flow, trans states, mystical states and sexually produced states – are neurobiologically very similar. They all generate high levels of alpha waves and produce a combination of five neurochemicals that are the most addictive and pleasurable drugs the human brain produces:
- dopamine
- norepinephrine
- serotonin
- endorphins
- anandamide

Alpha is 'the power of now', being here, in the present. It is the brain's resting state. Alpha waves aid overall mental coordination, calmness, alertness, mind/body integration and learning.

The first key to understanding happiness is that happiness doesn't live anywhere else but here and now. It can only be created in the present moment. So when we're waiting for something to change, we simply can't be happy, because we are constantly projecting ourselves into the future and looking for something 'other'.

Living in the future creates three feelings:

1. Fear

Living in the future forces us to unnaturally create a vision of what the future will look like. That image can either be positive or negative and has the power to imprison us. Even with positive images, the more we desire something, the more we become afraid that we will not get it. Instead of creating dreams, we create worries.

2. Absence

When we desire to be somewhere else and to experience something else, we are actually focusing on a feeling of absence. We create a deficiency, a sense of lack, a hunger, deprivation. When we focus on a lack of happiness, we create a lack of happiness. When we focus on a lack of wealth, we create more poverty. Focusing on any lack creates more lack. I meet so many people who are hungry for well-being. The problem is, they tell themselves they don't have well-being. They believe they need to do something in order to get somewhere better.

3. Rejection

If we are focused on a better, more colourful future, we are creating a constant rejection of the here and now. We believe tomorrow will be easier and happier, but that only makes the present moment more difficult and painful. All of us do this. As consciousness hacker Mikey Siegel says, 'Usually the part of us that is seeking is the part of us that is hurt.'[19]

The only way to experience happiness is to stop living in the future. The power of now can not only light us up with joy and acceptance but also truly create magic in our lives.

Why? Because when we truly accept what is, everything becomes a gift. And when we treat life and ourselves as a gift we open up whole new possibilities of existence.

My Miracle

When I was little, I believed everything was possible. I believed in magic and miracles. I believed I could become whoever I wanted to be. I danced, I sang, I painted. I acted, I played tennis and even basketball. I had so many dreams.

But the illnesses I suffered from, which I have discussed already, prevented me functioning normally for many years. I searched constantly for alternative healing methods. I couldn't accept that I would have to live a life full of pain and flare-ups until I died.

So I started to travel the world to see if anything or anyone could help me heal. And let me tell you, travelling was not easy. My luggage looked like a pharmacy. My friends had to send me my monthly dose of medication, ordered from America.

But I still was not ready to accept that this might be my life for ever. I just wasn't ready to give up.

One day, I was in northern Laos with my partner at the time. I remember that day like it was yesterday. Warm, bright, quiet. And my partner decided to break up with me.

Well, that was the cherry on top of the cake. It is funny how break-ups can break you more than years of physical suffering. I had had enough of this life. I remember I was so angry, so upset. Why is life treating me this way? It was the first time I actually spoke to the universe. Well, you can call it speaking or screaming depending on your definition.

I expressed myself very loudly. I said, 'Fine. You took everything I cared about. Now my life is yours. Give me whatever you want to give me. And if I am supposed to suffer like that for the rest of my life, well, so it goes. I let go. I am done with dreaming about a better future.'

I cried for days. I was so, so lost. And then things started to change.

I ended up at a meditation retreat in northern Thailand. It was two weeks after my breakdown. On the fourth day, I detached from my body. I was re-experiencing my body for the very first time. It felt as if I had entered my skin but it wasn't mine any more, it was just the vessel through which I could experience the world. Every sensation was extraordinary: touch, feel, smell, taste. I was noticing every single process and movement in my body, I started to perceive all the colours differently, I could even see the energy of plants and trees. I started to perceive reality completely differently. I started to have dreams about what was going to happen the next day. I didn't feel any pain; in fact I could simply switch pain off at will. It was as if I had come alive for the very first time. I stayed in this state for more or less ten days.

During this time, I experienced instant healing. I didn't know how it happened, but I knew that my disease was completely gone, for ever. I haven't taken any medication for the disease since.

Unexpected things started to come into my life at the speed of lightning. I realised that the universe wanted so much more for me than I could possibly imagine and that I was the only person standing in my way.

I felt this force guiding me, and my life transformed completely.

That day in Thailand, at the very moment when I had no more desire to heal, I was able to heal myself. When I stopped rejecting my sickness, when I fully accepted it and embraced it, that was when the magic returned to me. That was when I experienced the miracle I was looking for. That was when I actually broke free from that part of myself which was holding me back. It was that rejection that had been causing me the most discomfort.

See, you can't heal something that you are rejecting. When you reject your own disease, you actually block your body from initiating the healing process. You need to accept it in order for the unconscious mind to send the right instructions to your body but most importantly you need to love it, simply because it's yours, and you should never reject something that is yours. If you believe there is something wrong with you, no tool will help you. Letting go of desire, even the desire to heal, is the most powerful gift you can give to yourself. Only when we are ready to lose everything do we become ready to receive everything. Because the fear of loss will never allow us to have it all.

Be Here and Now

I have learned that the most beneficial state of consciousness is not an ecstatic state but a state of awareness, where you actually notice what is happening in the world around you and take it as it is without interpreting or grasping for something other. I believe that the only process of true healing, both mental and physical, is to be here and now, with full acceptance and love for yourself and for everything that is yours.

So, how can you always live in the present moment?

-   Set intentions without being attached to the result. When you get too attached to your own vision, you stop seeing other, potentially better opportunities and directions that arise. I always thought I would be healed by someone else. Only when I let go of that idea did something much better happen: I was able to heal myself.

- Whenever you feel you are starting to think about the future, ask yourself, 'What am I avoiding about the present moment?', 'How can I make this moment special?' For example, even when you are in a situation you don't want to be in, accept that everything is perfect as it is and make the maximum out of it. If you are in a place you don't want to be, make it special: put on some nice music, maybe light candles, read a book, write. Make this moment a memory.
- Whenever you feel you are not accepting yourself, ask this question: 'What if I will never be anything more than I am here and now? Could I be okay with that?'

Remember me in Laos, being able to accept myself, even with my illness. Gelong Thubten, a Buddhist monk, said in a conversation I had with him: 'When you have compassion for the parts of you that are hurt, resistance melts into joy.'

To put it simply, if you want to invest in your future, you need to invest in the now. Know that whoever you decide to be in this moment creates every moment of your future. Because your future is nowhere else than here and now.

Programming Happiness

Happiness is available to everybody here and now when we remove our expectations and stop waiting for it to happen to us. Happiness is unlimited. All you have to do is to make up your mind and choose it, over and over again, until it becomes your reality.

Dr Joe Dispenza explains that we train our body to create different molecules of emotions; feelings and emotions are a chemical record of past experiences. If we cultivate negative emotions over a long period of time, we create an automatic negative state of being. The chemistry of the body becomes not only a habit but also an addiction. We get addicted to guilt, shame, anger, sadness and so on. We have conditioned our body to be negative and when we feel its negative sensations we listen to them and go back to thinking negative thoughts. It becomes a loop. The only way to break it is to keep thinking positive thoughts, regardless of what we feel physically and of any external circumstances.

One positive thought won't change the state of our body from negative to positive; it takes time to change our emotional pattern and to reprogramme our body from reproducing the same neurochemicals. We need consistency and commitment to change; we need awareness of our tendencies and dedication to choosing to change our state of being in every moment. The good news is that just as negative emotions can become the operating system of your subconscious, so can the positive ones.

To begin to break ourselves free from feeling negative, we can start by training ourselves in thinking bigger and greater in every moment, and also in reminding ourselves how the good emotions feel by bringing back good memories from the past. For me, happiness is a mixture of love, trust, acceptance, joy and gratitude. If I find it hard to remember how happiness feels, I focus on those five feelings, which I know well, and try to feel at least one of them.

Positive feelings and happiness are our natural state, yet most of us have forgotten that. We often meet or speak to others to discuss our problems, more than we want to talk about our happiness. Ask yourself how often you share with your friends how happy you are.

Our Relationship With Ourselves

When we are unhappy, we have a tendency to think that we need someone to 'save' or 'complete' us.

We believe that love will make us happier. But, when we are unhappy, we can only attract another unhappy person. And a relationship of two unhappy souls, who want happiness from each other, is doomed to fail from the start. In order to enjoy a successful relationship, we have to care about our well-being first. What is truly best for ourselves is usually best for others too. What another person desires is not as essential as what we feel about it. We learn who we are through our relationship with everything that exists in our life. We must try different ways of existence in order to learn who we want to be.

Where Does Unhappiness Originate?

Where does unhappiness come from? It originates from rejecting who we really are and what we want within. Not what our ego wants, the desires of our heart. Unhappiness is usually a result of our attitude towards reality and the kind of perception we choose. We may believe that reality causes our unhappiness, but the truth is that it is our attitude to reality that dictates our feelings. Maharishi Mahesh Yogi, the father of Transcendental Meditation, which was developed in the early twentieth century, believed that bliss is a natural state of mind. As soon as we calm our mind and separate ourselves from our thoughts, our consciousness reverts automatically to its natural state of bliss and harmony. We can compare it to the ocean, which is rough and chaotic on the surface but contains peace and quiet within its depths.

If you are unhappy, it is because you are not living in alignment with yourself or your image of reality is inappropriate. It has nothing to do with not being in a relationship or not having the beautiful house you want. External factors are never the cause of our unhappiness. It is separation from the connection with ourselves and lack of alignment that make us unhappy.

Everything may be going well and yet you still feel unhappy, because your body has been conditioned to feel negative; vice versa, you may feel really happy despite unfavourable circumstances. If we calm our mind through meditation, our mood naturally comes back to its natural positive, peaceful state. We feel reconnected with ourselves and with everything around us. The more closely we approach ourselves, the more clearly we can hear our inner needs and, even louder, the voice of our intuition. When we open to that inward voice, it is very difficult to ignore it.

Travelling around various countries where poverty was ubiquitous, I met many people who possessed almost nothing, yet were much happier than me. When I went to India in 2006, I found the pervasive poverty that could be seen everywhere very hard to accept. But the more I stayed with the local people, the more clearly I could see that they enjoy everything life brings them – much more than me.

One day I was invited for lunch to a four-person family home. The tiny house where they all slept was about four square metres in size. This was staggering to me. I had a fantastic time with them and they hosted me generously; we ate and laughed and they were just so happy.

It took me years to fully grasp the significance of this experience. I travelled the world for over ten years looking for something, for myself. Yet I couldn't see what was in front of my eyes. I was not able to look within. I thought happiness had to be found. I tried to put conditions on it. I told myself, 'When I fall in love, I will be happy.' I wasn't. 'If I buy this or that, I will be happy.' I wasn't. And so on and so forth. Over and over, I would think I just hadn't yet found the stuff that brings happiness. I was mistaken. I could have got everything from the world and I'd still have been unhappy. Until I became the source of my happiness, my journeys were nothing but an escape from myself. I kept filling my reality with impressions, excitement just to feel I was alive. But this empty feeling inside me seemed to follow me wherever I went.

Inner-Connection

When I discovered Vipassana meditation, in northern Thailand, everything changed. I meditated for seven hours daily and I wrote. I was alone with myself. No telephone or computer, no friends or family, just me and my inner world.

So what happened then? It's difficult to describe: it was as if I saw myself and the world for the first time. I experienced total connection with everything else. I understood that the world and I are one. I started to feel the energy of everything around me, transcended from my body, and experienced everything more intensely, as if I had just been born. I had this impression that all the cells of my body were profoundly recovering. I felt connected with nature, with all the elements of the earth. But also, I felt connected to every single person as if they were part of me. I could feel everyone and everything so intensely that coming back to normal life was almost not an option. This experience was possible because I eventually opened up to myself and connected to myself. But the connection with everything that existed created at the same time a disconnection from everything that I knew. Disconnection from the past, from my old self, my old perception and my thoughts. I knew I wasn't the same person any more but I didn't know yet who and how I was. I felt unattached to most of the relationships in my life, but for the very first time, I did not feel alone and I did not feel separate.

I jumped off the cliff, trusting that I am not, and have never been, alone. I knew the whole universe was with me. I didn't have any blueprint as to what I was going to do or where I was going to be. I knew, however, that I was open to everything. My life surprised me greatly. I did not ask for anything, and I got much more than I could ever imagine. Much more than I would have planned or dreamt of. It was amazing.

But the most important result of that experience was that I stopped trying to run away from myself. I let go of any expectations I had about myself and about life in general. I committed to discovering who I truly was. I set out on a fascinating journey inwards. New visions of what I could do and how could I contribute in this life started to appear. My inner guidance sent me to the right places and situations. I felt synchronisation with what I truly desired and who I really was. From that moment on, I stopped planning my life. Everything started to clarify and appear by itself in the exact right moments. I lived in alignment with my intuition, trying not to dwell in the past or future. I started to implicitly trust life.

I am no longer afraid of dealing with challenging situations in my life, for I know they can help me to experience myself, to transform, to grow. I see them as opportunity, not a challenge. Yet, for some time, there were still moments when my mind rejected positive attitude, challenged my possibilities and tried to limit me. Then I felt unhappy again. Once more I doubted and felt unsure. Why?

Our higher Self contacts us through intuition. We feel we have to do something and go somewhere. If, however, we are filled with fearful thoughts, we suppress these feelings and then we feel misalignment. We feel sadness, uncertainty, disharmony. Our higher Self says one thing, the mind says something else.

Have you ever woken up with an amazing idea? You were convinced in that moment that it was the exact thing you had to do. You were completely open, excited, inspired and full of faith.

And then, a few minutes later, you started to doubt yourself. Your own thoughts started to sabotage you – 'How is it possible? How can it be done? Will I manage? Is it feasible at all?'

If it was not possible you wouldn't be able to feel that it was! As we have seen, it is only our mind, programmed to live in fear, that repeats old patterns and reacts with anxiety. Our job is not to decide how something is to be done, but what is to be done. The rest will follow – as soon as we are open to it. If we decide to take the leap because of our desire, we do not know when and how it will be fulfilled. We may be wonderfully surprised. We may plan something for next year but it might come true in a few days or weeks.

As we do not know how something will materialise in our life, we should never put any limit on it.

When I was halfway through my work on this book, I felt a great desire to get a massage. I was in Warsaw at the time and

I have never had a massage in that city before, so it was unclear where that desire came from. The same day, I got an invitation on Facebook from a woman I didn't know. I accepted it and the first thing I read on her page was an advert for massage in a parlour close to my flat. I phoned and made an appointment for the same day. I had a gut feeling that I was going to meet someone.

During the treatment I chatted with the therapist and we started talking about my book. The therapist was really keen on my ideas and suggested I could do weekly lectures or workshops on these topics. She knew a group of women who were interested in the subjects I was writing about.

Two weeks later, I started the workshops.

It was clear to me that it was my higher Self that had attracted me to that massage therapist at that point.

Inner Transformation

What if we were to start living in alignment with ourselves, with what we love doing? The world will listen and arrange the whole of reality for us. But the outer world can support us only when we start acting and creating our dreams. Unhappiness is when our heart fights with our mind. So, let's stop blaming the world when we do not follow our inner voice.

Everything starts from us, from the moment we make up our mind. The change must take place here and now. Let us listen to our higher Self. Let us not postpone our passions and our dreams. If we do not listen to the heart, it will start to shout. The less we listen, the louder it shouts, and we will need to invest more energy to fight that voice. There is nothing more exhausting than running away from oneself. So, let us be open to our inner callings. The more open we are, the more clearly we can see the sense of our existence, what we are to do, and the more easily we can manifest our dreams. The outer world depends on us, not vice versa. We are creators of our own reality. When we think the opposite, we lie to ourselves, we choose to not take responsibility for our life and we limit ourselves. We create borders that do not exist. Some people need an emotional shock, a break-up, a job loss, a slap from life in order to jump within. Others simply have to wake up. Yet, everything that happens to us happens from within us and pushes us towards that jump into the unknown, where we have to change our form, develop wings and become a butterfly. We don't know who we are when we jump; we need to just trust. But after discovering how high we can fly, it's as if someone let us out of a cage and showed us how beautiful the world is.

> In the time of unknowingness, when nothing can
> be seen, a new life is being created. It is under
> cover of darkness when the seed can crack open
> and take root. It is under cover of darkness
> when your soul can grow into a new life.

The actor, writer and storyteller Orson Bean shared a beautiful memory:

I remember Mr Bartlett. In biology class we discuss the transformation of a caterpillar into a butterfly. 'What is the process that goes on inside a cocoon?' he asks. 'Has anyone ever seen a picture of the insect at the halfway point between caterpillar and butterfly? Does anyone know what it looks like?' No one has or does.

The next week Mr Bartlett brings a cocoon to the classroom. We crowd around as he takes a razor blade and neatly slices it in two. The cocoon looks empty. 'There is nothing in there,' says one of the kids.

'Oh, it's in there,' says Mr Bartlett. 'It just doesn't have a shape right now. The living, organic material is spun right into the cocoon. The caterpillar is gone; the butterfly is yet to come.' We stare in wonder. 'Real transformation,' says Mr Bartlett, 'means giving up one form before you have another. It requires the willingness to be nothing for a while.'[20]

Recipes for Happiness

- Accept yourself and your desires. Accept not what your ego wants but what your heart desires. Unhappiness is rooted in disharmony; ignoring our true needs, acting against ourself and suppressing our intuition. When we follow our intuition instead, and honour our inner needs, we are guided by unseen forces to the exact right places and the exact right people.
- Put your heart into everything you do and stay fully present at every moment. If you are not fully present in everything you do, you will never feel that you did it well. Your mind will escape to wonder about the past or the future and you will not gain any satisfaction or fulfilment from what you have done. It will be a lost moment – as every moment when we are not fully present is lost because we are not really there. We can't receive anything from it and often it won't even stay in our memory. Always focus on the present moment rather than dwelling in the past or future, where most of our worries and fears live.

- Fall in love with the unknown. If we create a negative idea of the future we start to fear it. On the other hand, if we idealise our future, we will never be happy with what is here and now. We will become addicted to that vision of a 'better future' we have created in our mind and we will not appreciate everything that surrounds us now. The truth is, we never know what might happen. If I asked you to look back at the past year in your life, could you have imagined half of the things that have happened? Probably not! So simply stop trying to figure out what the future might bring. Let life surprise you. Happiness is not hidden in the past or future. It is here and now. It is enough to reach for it.
- Don't do anything you don't want to do and whatever you do, don't search for gratification.
  When we expect gratification, we are not doing the thing for ourselves; therefore, we are not in alignment with ourselves. Have you ever tried to do something for yourself and still sought approval from others? You simply wouldn't do it. You would be proud of yourself instead. We never know how good we are unless we are our best and you can only be your best at things you truly desire.
- Don't wait to be happy; the circumstances will never be just right. During the week, we wait for the weekend. At the weekend, we think about the week to come. At work, we look forward to our holidays. We are in a permanent state of waiting. Let us give that up and be happy here and now. Let's enjoy today instead of waiting for a better tomorrow.
- Cultivate a positive attitude. When we are used to spending time feeling negative emotions, our body literally gets

addicted to feeling bad. We reinforce it by listening to sad music, consuming negative information from the media, complaining to others about our problems, sympathising with others' unhappiness and so on. We nourish our bad feelings daily and we are surprised that we can't overcome them.

- To start to experience positive emotions instead we have to be aware of the negative thoughts and behaviours we are creating and let go of them. Have only positive conversations about your own life. Share your gratitude and appreciation for things. Watch comedies and listen to positive music. If you catch yourself having negative thoughts, change them. The change will appear all around you.

Fifteen Steps to Realising That You Are Happy Already

1. Always want to be here and now. What can you do to make THIS moment special?

2. Give yourself some credit for who you are today. For all your efforts, all your determination, all your strength, for all your patience, for all your dreams. If you had to give advice to yourself ten years ago, what would it be? What advice will you give to yourself today?

3. Don't beat yourself up for the mistakes you have made. Like Confucius said: Our greatest glory is not in never falling, but in rising every time we fall. Stand up and stand up tall. Every morning is a new beginning and today is the first day of the rest of your life. Who do you choose to be?

4. Love and appreciate yourself. You are ideal and unique. There is no other person in this universe who is like you.

You are your own greatest gift just as you are. What are three things you love about yourself?

5. Take action. You can't expect your reality to change if you are not ready to change your actions. What are you going to do differently today?

6. Remember that happiness is not conditioned. It is us who condition it. Make a decision to feel happy here and now, regardless of your circumstances. You do not depend on the world; the world depends on you. How do you choose to feel right now? Say it.

7. Be grateful for what you have. For all the stars in the sky. For every sunbeam on your face. For every single smile you have given to the world. Gratitude holds enormous power. What are you grateful for today?

8. Always focus on positive thoughts. Bad thoughts attract even more negativity. Replace each negative thought with a positive memory from the past. Learn to generate happiness at will. What is your positive memory from today?

9. Don't take anything personally. People's emotions are only the mirror of what they have within. What matters is not someone's behaviour but how you react to it. To what did you choose to react positively today?

10. Feel today how would you like to feel tomorrow. Sometimes you can't change your situation immediately, but you can make up your mind to feel as if you had. How would you feel if your dreams came true right now? Feel it.

11. Stay open. When we are closed, nothing can get out and nothing can get in. We can't give and we can't receive. We create walls around ourselves. Happiness is born in the flow of giving and receiving. Do you choose to stay open?

12. Every single day, give something to someone else. A compliment, a smile, a helping hand, a gift, a surprise. When we give to others we give to ourselves. What are you going to give today?

13. Take off your mask. When you put on the mask, you not only hide yourself but also you reject who you are. You stop others from seeing you. When you show yourself fully, you might be rejected, but it is much worse to be rejected for who you are NOT, than for who you truly are. It is our own rejection that is the most painful. Which part of yourself you will show to others today?

14. Stay curious about yourself. You can't discover who you truly are unless you accept that you might not know it all in the first place. Find comfort in the mystery. Stay open to the possibilities of who you might become without planning. You might surprise yourself. What new thing are you going to discover about yourself today?

15. Marry yourself! Don't cheat on yourself any more. Be with yourself for all the right (and wrong) reasons. For better or worse. Celebrate your relationship with yourself. Whatever you do, don't beat yourself up; accept or love all the 'unwanted' parts of yourself as well as the good ones. Cherish yourself today as you would cherish a spouse. What are you going to do for yourself today?

Happiness Hacks

Write down five positive situations from your life when you felt wildly happy and for which you are grateful. Then, lie down somewhere comfortable and imagine these situations once more, one by one. Recall how you felt. Devote about five minutes to each situation. Learn to recall them at will. These are going to be your Happiness Hacks: from now on, each time you discover a negative thought in your mind, recall one of these situations. Recall the feeling involved in it. Observe your stress fading. Observe how you become happy again. Teach your body to feel happiness at will.

When You Feel Sad

Happiness is not getting what you want but wanting what you get. Whenever you feel sad it means either that you are misaligned and you are not following your truest desires, or you have imagined a certain scenario for your experience and life is not matching what you have imagined; therefore you feel disappointed.

If you are misaligned, you probably know already in which areas you are going against yourself but you are too afraid to make a change.

Nothing will help you to feel better until you change or leave the situation that is not right for you.

If you are unhappy and disappointed, ask yourself the questions below. Reflect for a few minutes on each question or write down your reflections:

1. What am I expecting right now? From myself, from my experience, from another person.
2. Why am I expecting this? What am I hoping this will bring me/make me feel like?
3. Could I generate this state regardless of external conditions? Could I be happy with what I am receiving from

life here and now, assuming that everything serves my greatest good?

4. What is the worst that can happen if my expectations can't be fulfilled; can I be okay with it?
5. What does my current situation offer me?

For example:

I am disappointed I haven't met anyone yet on my holiday in Greece. I was hoping to meet people to have some more fun, make new friends, be social, feel more alive. Can I feel more alive by myself? Sure, I just need to be my own best company and organise some fun activities. The worst that can happen is that I will be all by myself the whole time. Can I be okay with that? Yes! This situation offers me lots of time to reflect, meditate, read. It calms and slows me down. Perhaps this is exactly what I need right now.

Be grateful for whatever you receive, remove your expectations from everything and open up to whatever surprise life is ready to offer you. When we don't hold any expectations we are much more likely to be positively surprised about situations we are exposed to and, most important of all, we are ready to receive them. That's why the best things happen when we don't expect it: everything simply becomes a gift.

9

Why Are We Afraid of Loving?

*Fear itself is more frightening than
that which we are afraid of.*

•

*We can't be afraid of love, we can only be afraid of
an idea of love that our mind has created.
But since the mind can't love, it can't know what love is.
Because true love can be only felt, not known.*

What Do I Feel When I Say 'Love'?

When I asked myself this question for the first time, I wanted to say: Love is good and it brings me positive thoughts and associations. It makes me feel safe, secure and empowered. Love inspires me and holds me. It makes me smile when I wake up. It makes me laugh when I am afraid. It makes me a cup of tea when I am sick.

Sadly that was not what love used to mean to me.

I felt so betrayed, rejected and hurt by the love I experienced early on. I wanted to run away from it, somewhere, anywhere far. I became afraid of love. I wanted to hide from it. Push-and-pull relationships and bullying, dictating behaviours and disputes were my reality every day. So when I heard the word 'love', I would think: love hurts, love fights, love punishes, love rejects, love controls, love disempowers, love disrespects and love belittles.

I wanted love to be good and bring me positive thoughts and associations, but it didn't. Unfortunately, many people as well as me have negative associations when it comes to love. Childhood memories, family relationships and school experiences are often painful and difficult. Even if we don't experience violence, we might experience a lack of support, understanding or affection, which would make our sense of love insensitive, cold and closed.

If we don't realise the negative associations we make with love, we will keep operating through our unconscious beliefs and keep re-creating painful experiences. And so this is how the love will show up for us, not only in our relationships with others but also in the most important relationship we have – with ourselves. We will treat ourselves in the very same way we learned to be treated by others. If I believe that love hurts, fights, punishes, rejects, controls, disempowers, disrespects and belittles, it means that I will be hurting, punishing, reject-ing, controlling, disempowering, disrespecting and belittling myself. If I didn't receive much attention or affection as a child, I will most likely crave it. I will unconsciously copy the patterns of behaviour I experienced from others and use them towards myself. And because our external reality is just an extension of who we are, I will attract partners who will give me the exact same love I give to myself – or the exact same lack of it.

How Do We Avoid Love?

The universe 'replies' to our thoughts. Our beliefs about love become our reality and if we are afraid of love, our subconscious protects us from it. If we do not believe in love, we will never experience it. If we assume that love will hurt us, that will come true. We will not only create situations in which people will hurt us, but what's worse, we will keep hurting ourselves. Life will reflect our definitions and adapt to what we believe. We attract exactly what we fear. So, if we fear losing love, that will be our lot.

Consider what thoughts come into your head when you think about love. How do you react when you see a love-struck couple? What are your first associations or spontaneous feelings?

Are they distrust, suffering, disappointment, illusion, lies, limitation, pain, betrayal? If any of these words are what came to your mind, that's great – you already know the name of your problem, and that means you can solve it.

The only way to liberate ourselves from this loop is to re-create our own definition of love and decide how we choose to experience it. What helped me was to disassociate my childhood pain from love and create a new association. If we change how we perceive what we are afraid of, our fear dissolves.

My change didn't happen overnight. My self-defence mechanisms prevented me for many years from being hurt by love again. The bigger the commitment I felt I was making, the greater was the likelihood that I would end up in a flight or panic response, creating various stories and scenarios in my mind, that held me back from fully stepping in and opening up to receiving love.

The more powerful the love we feel, the greater the fear of being hurt by it. The greater the fear, the stronger the activation of a 'rescue programme' designed to push away what we fear.

If we fear rejection, we might find ourselves doing the reject-ing. If we fear being hurt, we might become the attacker. If we fear being deceived, we have likely started lying to ourselves or others. All these mechanisms are designed to protect us. We hide inside ourselves, we withdraw, we shut down. We pull back behind a shield, locking in our emotions, problems, blockages and illnesses, preventing anything from leaving our body, effectively imprisoning ourselves.

Michael A. Singer in his book *The Untethered Soul* describes how this action closes our energy centres. We become unreceptive and insensitive. We would rather defend the concepts and beliefs created by our protective mechanisms than our bodies. If we lock our illnesses inside ourselves they can only worsen. If we constantly protect ourselves, we can never be free, we will never grow, and we can never fully receive.

Love and self-sabotage

What are some of your self-sabotaging programmes? I'll tell you about some that I created and experienced for myself. Believe me, my creativity doesn't only shine through my work, it also shines in all my subconscious creations! My mind was very creative coming up with all the techniques I would employ to push people away.

The first programme I created was 'to run for the hills', which is a flight response. I would turn to it whenever I was triggered by a situation that connected me to unexpressed or unreleased energies from the past that might activate a fear of rejection. Unconsciously I believed that if I rejected first I wouldn't be rejected. I became the very source of rejection, not only of the other person but also of myself.

Everyone's deepest desire is to love and be loved, but if we're paralysed by fear we don't allow ourselves to either give or receive it. We run away. Have you ever experienced being triggered by someone and thinking about jumping on the first plane or train to leave the situation? Well, this is exactly how this programme works. And the only way to free ourselves from it is to realise we are in a programme and to consciously decide to let go of it.

Another strategy I created could be called 'looking for problems'. I would look for small issues in my relationships and then make big problems out of them. I would start to criticise and blame my partner for my unhappiness, frustration, or irritation. I would blame him for not making me happy. I would focus on every little thing that bothered me and constantly look for conflicts. I did it because I felt insecure and I was looking for confirmation and reassurance that the other person loved me. I was unable to be honest with myself about it so, rather than taking responsibility for my own experiences, I would try to convince myself that the relationship was not working.

If that technique didn't 'work' with my partner I would try the 'attack him' technique. It is a more violent version of the one above. I'd literally try to pick a fight, to shake him, to feel his emotions, to see if he still cared about me. I'd try to provoke a reaction because I wanted someone to fight for me. I was so insecure in my own skin that I would do anything to draw out someone's feelings, in the hope that I might be able to feel my own. Sadly, it only brought me more separation.

If my partner was unresponsive to these techniques above I might try to 'numb myself'. I started creating an idea that I felt less and less, to desensitise myself. I would start to doubt my love and, through the numbness, start to lose the physical attraction I once had to my partner. All of this was to numb my own pain. To protect myself from being hurt meant to prevent myself from feeling my own pain. I would close myself off and start to build walls around me to prevent my partner from getting in. When my partner commented that I was closed, I would ignore it and remain in denial. I literally couldn't feel my own closure. I'd start to believe that the relationship might be over because I didn't feel anything any more. But it was only a way to escape. Sooner or later when I opened up again, all of those feelings would come out and I would realise all the lies I was telling myself. But sometimes it was too late.

Another self-sabotaging belief I had was 'it's too good to be true'. I was so attached to what had happened to me in the past that I struggled to believe that my future could be any different. My main mantra in this programme was: 'Here I go again!' I believed I didn't deserve happiness, I was not worthy or loveable. My beliefs often became a self-fulfilling prophecy as I was creating the reality I feared the most. No matter how wonderful my partner was, and how much he said he loved me, I never believed him. It was never enough to convince me that the reality was different to the one I was holding in my mind. In this programme we simply stop believing in the relationship. We close ourselves into the dark, pessimistic vision of our future that we are creating from a place of fear.

Fears can force us to flee from ourselves; we reject, harm or deny ourselves in the process. For me, love is holding someone in my arms when they are trying to run away from themselves. For me, love is reassurance in the face of doubt. For me, love is to be the truth in the face of self-deception. For me, love is to stand in certainty while the other pushes me away. For me, love is to see through the criticism and the blame for the lies that they are. Love is to realise that everything else is fear. Love is to keep my heart open, even if everything else seems to close. No matter what.

It is relatively easy to lead a quiet, stress-free life when we are single, without any commitments. It can be easier than investing into and building a relationship. Yet, what outcomes can we expect from this choice? I would use the justification of being single being easier to bury my desire for love deeper and deeper until I stopped hearing it at all. Then, I could claim that I did not need it.

I persuaded myself until I started to believe that I didn't need love; that love was ephemeral and that I was better off alone. But the truth was, I closed myself off to love in order to protect myself. If we are closed, we are unable to receive what other people want to give us but also we can't receive our own love. If we close ourselves off, we not only block potential connection with another person, but also with anyone else – including ourselves.

Only among our loved ones do we get the opportunity to show our true nature, our real face; who we are underneath the mask we have created for ourselves. Have you noticed how your behaviour differs when you are with your parents or partner from when you spend time with your friends? Perhaps with your family or partner you shout, get offended, use an abrupt tone, burst into tears, sulk or otherwise behave unpleasantly. You may think, 'This is not really me; it's them making me like this.' The truth, though, is the opposite: This is exactly who you are. What are you going to do with it?

It is in these very situations that we have the opportunity to see and to work on ourselves, on the person we want to become. We can work through our blocks, our inner fear, our ego, and discover all the unexpressed emotions hiding in us.

I deprived myself of the possibility of love because I was not able to love myself. And I believed that it was simply bad luck that I hadn't met the 'right' person. Except that there is no such thing as bad luck. I was attracting exactly what I was ignoring in myself. I was not willing to see parts of myself that were screaming to be voiced. As Einstein put it: 'Insanity is repeating the same mistakes and expecting different results.'

Every human being is born and dies with a deep need for love. It is not only our most basic need but also the fuel for all creation. Rejecting love means rejecting our greatest gift. If we are not able to create something in our life, we push it away. Our subconscious mind sabotages our life. When we deprive ourselves of love, we are not able to experience ourselves fully. We are unable to tap into our biggest potential and driving force. Love is the most powerful energy of creation. Anything we do, we do either from love, or out of a cry for love.

The kind of love we carry within ourselves is the love we are going to experience in our reality. The way you love yourself will be the exact way in which you will be loved by others.

I have realised that we all naturally love; and if we do not live in our natural state, we suffer. We go against our true nature.

Ask yourself: How do you love yourself?

Love is not for the chosen ones. Love is from and for those who have chosen it.

Beliefs about Love

Write on a sheet of paper the foundational beliefs you hold about love?

What deeply held beliefs are shaping your life? What are your thoughts when you see couples in love? What opinions about love are recorded in your memory?

Who was the first person to express these opinions? Are those beliefs yours or given to you by your relatives or friends? Do they move you at a deep level or are they holding you back? Are your beliefs empowering or rather limiting? Are these beliefs the ones you would like to have?

10

The Fear of Separation

Separation exists in order to connect everything.

•

Sometimes loving means creating and maintaining
a relationship, and sometimes it means ending it.
That's why the most important commitment in
a relationship is not to a person but to love itself.

•

The main purpose of our soul is to evolve as creator.
The main purpose of a relationship is to reflect
to us how much we've evolved. The main
purpose of love is to keep us evolving.

Every relationship contributes to our life. What's important
is not how long it lasts but what you get from it, what your
individual experience is. In fact, the most important gift is
to experience oneself in every moment and live accordingly.
Quite often, we fear relationships because of the possibility
that they will end; but the end of a relationship makes us
introduce some changes into our life. That break-up, that
suffering gives us the motivation to care about ourselves
more. We have to leave our comfort zone, and so we undergo
a transformation. Every destruction is a chance to build
something new. Like Nicholas Sparks beautifully said: 'The
emotion that can break your heart is sometimes the very one
that heals it.'[21]

A separation might make you become stronger, more independent, and more conscious of what you need. According to statistics, more divorced people than people who are married achieve professional success and establish their own businesses. Why? Because divorced people have consciously decided to take control over their life, they have chosen to take personal responsibility for their own happiness. They have overcome their fear. The point is not that everyone should get divorced, but that no one should be limited by their relationships.

When one door closes, another one opens up – whether we can see it or not is another question! – but everything ends up making sense eventually. Everything is a part of a wider plan. Let's remember that only by looking backwards can we make connections and understand the purpose of past events. When a seemingly negative event happens, you don't know what positive effect it might bring. That's why it's wise not to judge anything too early.

Therefore, why be afraid of relationships or of them ending? There is no need to be afraid of change or of new people entering our lives. Each of them brings us something new – and to some extent, as we have seen, they reflect ourselves back to us. Every person plays the role of a mirror in our life. If only we could grasp that! No longer would there be any disappointments. We would know that no matter how long or short a relationship is, its purpose was to show us something important about ourselves.

If we fear separation, sooner or later we will attract it. Our subconscious will sabotage our thoughts, words and deeds, making it inevitable. We expect from our partner exactly what we expect from ourselves; so fear of separation can mean that we are not able to provide for ourselves, that we are separated from our own needs or desires. Feel whole in who we are.

We fear separation from others only when we feel separated from ourselves.

While sometimes we are afraid of love and connection, at other times we fear loneliness or solitude the most and so will stay in a relationship at all costs. We become dependent on the other person for what we cannot give ourselves. Most of the time we are no longer really in a relationship with our partner but just in a relationship with our own issues. We look at the other person through our own prism. And we often stay in a relationship not because we love the person, but for love of the benefits of the relationship.

For many people, having a relationship is a condition of things like being happy, being successful and feeling safe. 'I will be happy when I meet someone,' we often think. 'Everything in my life will fall into place as soon as I fall in love.'

But why isn't your life complete, successful or safe, now? Often we don't ask ourselves this question. We build our reality upon conditional assumptions to avoid taking responsibility for how we feel.

During the first few months, with our hormones bubbling away, we may be on cloud nine – but what happens when after a short while the excitement fades (as it always does) and we find ourselves back in the same state? We may start to find reasons for our unhappiness in the other person. We may foster and encourage feelings of isolation and loneliness in the relationship.

Paradoxically, sometimes we feel more lonely in a relationship than when we are single. We run away from our partner to talk about our problems with others. We highlight with metaphorical red markers everything we don't like and want to change about them and the relationship, belabouring the problems ad nauseam. Longing for intimacy with our partner may become yearning for intimacy with anybody. We run away from the empty space that is created between us and our partner. Yet we are afraid to leave that space definitively, for the very thought we could leave evokes a tiger's zeal to fight – for something that might not even exist.

Everything evolves. Someone who was an ideal partner for you two years ago might not be the right person for you now. Why? Because you have changed. Your partner may not have evolved in the same way or direction as you. You may now have totally different expectations, and both of you may need someone else in order to keep developing.

Breaking up with your partner does not mean losing love. We shouldn't be afraid of that, for love is eternal. The body passes away, the consciousness lives for ever. By loving someone and sending that energy into the universe, we in fact send it to ourselves. That is why we should send as much as we can. If we close ourselves to love because of the fear of being hurt, we make others incapable of loving us. We paradoxically believe that the other person will come, heal and unjam us; but when we have blockages within ourselves, we block out everything around us too.

Evolution and Eternal Energy

It is a false assumption that love is ephemeral. Human feelings change and transform but love is a pure form of energy and, once sent out into the universe, exists for ever.

Have you ever met an ex-partner after many years apart and you still have those butterflies in your stomach? That is the eternal energy of love.

Another false assumption is that love hurts. Love never hurts. What hurts is our will to possess and control. The way we perceive love and its end. The image we create in our mind about how love should be.

As soon as we understand that love does not end, that once offered and received it will exist as energy in us for ever, we will understand that it cannot hurt. We do, though, need to activate that energy and explore its depths. Some people need many relationships to explore this; for others, it takes just one relationship for a lifetime. It is very individual; some people evolve so quickly that they need many different partners to reflect this, others will find one person who evolves with them at the same speed and in the same direction, and others again need to attract similar partners and experiences over and over again to reflect where they haven't been evolving. Again, we can't witness where we are at without seeing our reflection in another person, our mirror.

Relationships are not there to protect the self-image that we have cultivated about ourselves but to destroy it and to show us what lies underneath.

The main purpose of our soul is to evolve as creator. The main purpose of a relationship is to reflect to us how much we've evolved. The main purpose of love is to keep us evolving. Love is the fuel for our growth. We must give it and be filled with it endlessly, rather than focus on how to keep someone at our side. Sometimes loving means creating and maintaining a relationship, and sometimes it means ending it. That's why the most important commitment in a relationship is not to a person but to love itself. When we deprive ourselves of love, we are not able to experience ourselves fully and to tap into our biggest creative potential. Love is the most powerful energy of creation.

Why then, instead of enjoying the fact that we have fallen in love, do we fear that the chosen person will leave us? We are afraid of separation, of losing physical contact and consequently of losing love. We are afraid of it because we don't set our love free. And love that is not free is not love at all. It is just an idea of love. An idea that we all desire, but that at the same time we are all terrified of – we think that it might change us, or limit us, lessen us, control us, imprison us or hurt us. Well, all of the above can be true, if we create them and let them be our reality. But trust me, if your heart is filled with love towards everyone and everything, you will never feel limited, lessened, controlled, imprisoned or hurt. You will be free from your own limitations and judgement.

Let me share with you a story to illustrate how I uniquely created it for myself.

I fell in love. After spending some beautiful moments together we were presented with a choice; we could either wait to see how things might unfold, or jump from the proverbial cliff and commit to being with each other come what may.

We threw ourselves off the cliff, with the belief that everything can be gained from an attitude of 'all-in'.

But, as we've seen, the bigger the commitment, the greater the potential to end up in a flight or panic response. The more powerful the love we feel, greater our fear of losing it. In trying to avoid this fear, we can end up either rejecting the relationship or trying to control it.

I tried both.

On the one hand, I started to use various self-sabotaging mechanisms, creating different stories and scenarios in my mind that were supposed to protect me from potential suffering by pushing away the potential of the love that lay before me.

On the other hand, I began to close down my feelings. I created an idea of the 'ideal' love and the 'ideal' partner that I had always dreamt of. I tried to control the love by defining how it should be, how my partner should behave and how he should feel at every moment.

Objectively the relationship was great. We moved in together, we started to work on some projects together, we travelled around the world. We shared so many passions and dreams that were in true alignment. We had the same kind of lifestyle and liked the same things. Every day we felt more strongly how deep this love and connection was between us.

But I started to feel unsettled, unsatisfied, unhappy and somehow blocked. And I couldn't put a finger on why I was feeling this way. Nothing made sense. I started to look for reasons to explain my low mood around my relationship. I started to get demanding, controlling and dependent. I really didn't like how I was feeling. I started to question him and our relationship itself. Every time the reality would not follow the rules created by my mind, I would get upset, angry, disappointed, disconnected. 'This is not what I signed up for,' I would think to myself.

One morning when I woke up I went into a meditative state and I suddenly saw things with full clarity. The understanding didn't come to me from a long process of thinking but from silencing my mind. I burst into tears. I saw how much I was limiting not only him and our relationship, but also our love. I saw the walls I had built around love by trying to limit it to an idea that would make me feel safe. And living in this idea was holding me back from fully stepping in and opening up to it. I become conditioned. Framed. Closed.

My closure was preventing the possibility of expressing or receiving love fully, feeling it, seeing it and letting it be free.

I thought I was getting what I wanted, but actually I was constantly pushing my partner away. I was trying to decide how he should be and what he should feel, not allowing him to be who he truly is and, even worse, not loving him for it. My love was conditional.

If we ask for love and we want it to be a certain way, we create expectations that push our loved one away. We construct walls around them. We don't allow them to be who they are. We might think the other person is not being affectionate, open or loving enough, but that is simply because what we are communicating with our attitude is: 'I will not love you if you are not like I told you to be.'

How can the other person be open, loving, caring or secure if this is the message we are giving them? How many of us are criticising our loved ones? How many of us love them conditionally? Is that the type of love we would like to experience and create in our lives?

We think we love but we don't really, because we are constantly criticising and judging it in our head. We are focusing on our list of needs, trying to pack our partners into boxes that meet our expectations. We create recipes for each other for how to make us satisfied. But why are we not satisfied in the first place? Why won't we take responsibility for our own satisfaction?

By not accepting love for what it is, we are not allowing love to be there at all. We are pushing it away.

In my extraordinary realisation that morning, when I was finally able to see more clearly what was happening and what I was doing, with tears in my eyes, I looked at my partner and said: 'I set you free.'

I had taken complete responsibility for what I had been creating, and suddenly we reconnected to each other in a whole new way.

I realised that the control I had been trying to exert over him and our love was the same control I was performing on myself. Those walls I was building around us were not only limiting him but also limiting who I was. The conditions, ideas and expectations I had were completely constricting and repressing his, and my, natural expression. The unhappiness I was feeling was coming from my own limitations, restrictions and conditions with myself. Conditions for my own self-love. And how can I love somebody else if I can't love myself?

By setting him free, I set myself free. In that moment I not only accepted and saw him but I also accepted and saw myself. I no longer had to feel the fear of losing control because control was no longer necessary. It didn't matter any more how long the relationship would last; every day of experiencing it became a beautiful gift.

Removing expectations about love might be the biggest sign of true love, because true love is free.

That morning was the morning when I started a new relationship. A new relationship with myself. That was the moment that I actually really jumped off the cliff. I let go of my need for control and the idea of love I had created and I decided to completely surrender to the unknown. I chose to trust and to believe instead of creeping forward fearfully. I opened myself fully to the possibility of love.

I became free.

Most of the time we are not afraid of separating from the person, but rather from our idea of them. The image of the future we have created in our minds. The vision we have projected onto them. What do you want from this person that you believe you can't create yourself?

The essence of a harmonious relationship rests on sharing plentitude, not on completing someone else. If we look for someone to genuinely share our happiness with, we will meet a person who wants the same. There will be no expectations, no conditions and no disappointment. You will be able to create a real treasure. This new relationship will give you wings and will teach both of you to fly. Together and next to each other. As Victoria L. White writes:

> Eventually, you stop needing to have the experience of heartbreak. And you stop needing to have the experience of heartbreak when you realise you are already whole. If you already love, no one can come into your life and take away the love you've cultivated and become. When you go into a relationship whole and you decide to end it, you leave the relationship whole, when it was truly based in love. No one can deplete you of love when you have the realisation you are already love.

Separation exists in order to connect everything.

Eye Gazing

Find either a partner or a friend, and sit with them in a quiet environment. Sit facing each other and look into each other's eyes for five minutes without any interruption. The first part of this exercise is to notice what are you feeling, what emotions go through your body. Does it make you uncomfortable or shy? Do you feel like laughing or perhaps crying? What emotions are rising in you?

In the second part, try to guess what the person in front of you is experiencing and feeling. What is your impression of them? Do you think he/she is comfortable? What emotions do you feel rising in him/her?

After five minutes, give each other a big hug and share your experiences with each other.

11

The Fear of Betrayal

No one can ever cheat on you;
we can only ever cheat on ourselves.

•

Challenging situations in life show up so you can challenge
your own reaction to it and your own perception of it.
And when you can see every situation simply as an
opportunity, you won't find it challenging any more.

I was always afraid to trust others and to trust life in general. The insecurity that was born out of this lack of trust would not only cloud all the positives in my relationships but would also actually magnetise the negative scenarios I was afraid of. These struggles, challenges and problems were often similar to each other. It was almost as if the people who I was attracting had the same special code to activate my deepest wounds.

This topic preoccupied me for a long time. How could I finally relax and feel secure in my relationships – and, most importantly, how could I feel more secure with myself? How could I see more widely, see beyond?

And then a friend of mine said to me: 'You are the most super-chilled, patient, easy-going, funny, spontaneous person ever. But in relationships you don't act like that. If only you would let go of whatever conditioned you to be like this with your partners!'

It shocked me. I had never considered that how I felt was conditioned by something I had not yet seen. I would just beat myself up for being so far off who I wanted to be.

I started to reflect on this idea of conditioning. Started to study every single relationship in my life, including the one I had with my parents. I started to find commonalities and links between them, and what they all had in common was lack of trust.

One day I asked my mum what she was most afraid of and she said to me: 'I was always the most afraid of betrayal. I've been afraid of it ever since I was pregnant with you.'

I realised now that I had carried my mother's trauma with me my entire life without knowing it. All the emotions the mother experiences when she is pregnant – including shock, trauma, grief, fear – are felt by the child. They are then imprinted in the child's body memory and create the reality accordingly. In my case I had attracted many betrayals, in different forms, through different people in all areas of my life, both professional and personal. Each one only deepened my fear of betrayal.

The worst betrayal was when I was cheated on in my first relationship. I will never forget the pain I felt the moment I found out about it, on my twentieth birthday. The pain penetrated all my cells and even though my boyfriend really wanted us to stay together, I knew it would never be possible.

I started to crave a commitment, crave a promise that no one would ever do that to me again. But sadly no words or actions were ever enough to rebuild my trust in love. The fear of betrayal would not only look for any negative sign or suspicious behaviour in all my relationships, it would also create all sorts of negative scenarios in my mind that would then become a self-fulfilling prophecy. This fear was buried so deeply inside me that I didn't even realise how much I was sabotaging all my relationships. I simply didn't trust anyone. This fear was so uncomfortable, so unpredictable, so uncontrollable that it would never allow me to enjoy any of my relationships. It would never allow me to let anyone in. I disliked myself for feeling this way and I would do anything to stop that feeling. Including ending the relationship when things got too uncomfortable.

But running from the situations that could potentially hurt me was not only running away from my fears and insecurities; it was also running away from life, running away from love and running away from myself. I only understood years later that every person who was given the code to touch my deepest wounds was there to help me to heal them. The question was, was I ready to heal them? Was I ready to confront and to release my fear or would I rather run away from it for the rest of my life? Only, when we run away, life just sends us bigger and bigger arrows pointing out our wounds until we can not ignore them any more.

And then, many years later, I was cheated on again. This time it was much worse: months of lying, hiding another relationship, making me think it was all in my head and finally making me feel guilty for causing it. My greatest fear had manifested itself – but not to hurt me, to heal me this time. I allowed myself to feel the entire pain, grief, anger, injustice and betrayal. I felt completely broken for weeks, I had a nervous breakdown. I cried for days and days. Only now, I knew that in order to heal myself I had to meet my greatest fear face to face. So I surrendered to it. Gosh it was painful! And at the same time it was the greatest gift I could ever receive. Why? Because it allowed me to release the fear that would never allow me to trust love, that would never allow me to trust anyone, including myself. Thanks to this experience, I met myself again; I opened up more than ever before, I became more confident, I fell in love with life and most of all I learned to trust. I learned to trust that every single experience in life serves my greatest good. I saw, finally, that after every storm there is a peaceful clear sky. I survived facing my greatest fear, and so I had nothing to fear any more. I was free.

Cheating on Ourselves

The truth is, no one can ever cheat on you; we can only cheat on ourselves. People don't belong to us and they never will. There are no words or actions that can guarantee that someone will stay with us, love us for ever and be loyal to us. Everything can change.

We can't predict if our partner will choose someone else or look for a different experience. If someone cheats on us it doesn't mean they don't love us, it only means they don't love themselves. They're looking for confirmation from other people of how good they are. They need validation from more than one person because they don't accept themselves.

We can't ever be in control of what someone will do. However, we can choose our reaction to it and be our best selves in every single moment. That is in our power. Challenging situations in life show up so we can challenge our own reaction to them and our own perception of them.

When we can see every situation simply as an opportunity, we won't find it challenging any more. And if we live in alignment with our heart, we can only ever feel good about ourselves. It is when we deny our desires, our heart's needs and our intuition that we cheat – on ourselves. When I met the second partner who cheated on me, after our second date I felt very sad for no reason. I called my best friend and said to her: *I don't feel this will continue, something is off. I don't think I will see him again.* But I did. I pushed back that first instinct that something was wrong and I kept seeing him. My gut feeling was getting stronger and stronger but I convinced myself that I was paranoid. On paper everything looked fine.

I realised that I didn't have to trust him, I had to trust myself.

To give any relationship a real chance,
you don't have to trust your partner,
you have to trust your heart,
because your heart will never guide you
towards something that is not good for you.

When you trust yourself, you don't need others to tell you what to do, you make your own decisions based on your instant feelings and not your changeable mind. When you trust yourself, you don't ignore yourself, you don't avoid yourself, you don't quiet yourself – you listen to your inner guidance and you honour your heart's whispers. When you trust yourself, you don't blame yourself for any situation, you know that whatever you attract in your life always serves you. When you trust yourself, you don't reject any aspect of yourself, you own it. Because you know that everything that you experience yourself allows you to discover and create yourself even more. Every new experience becomes a new substance to create with. When you trust yourself, you do not fear acting wrongly, you know that whatever you do or say, however you act, you are always being a blessing for yourself and others and serving everyone's growth. When you trust yourself, you don't distrust others, and you don't distrust life. You welcome every experience with open arms, knowing that everything comes from you and in fact reflects you. And finally, when you trust yourself, you don't need to know, you simply trust the unknown, seeing that everything happens in the exact right place and moment in time. The best moment for you.

In any relationship, we crave to be reassured that the love will last, that it won't hurt us, that it won't abandon us. Sometimes we are so desperate to know if something will last or not that we are ready to end it ourselves just to get an answer. The real security is not born from getting answers to our questions, in being reassured by words and actions but simply from being able to trust the unknown and staying curious about every moment to come. Sometimes knowing when something will end is easier than not knowing how long something will last. It gives us an illusion of control. An illusion of having an answer. We prefer to pick a negative scenario that is sure, rather than a positive one that is unsure. But, what if we will never know? Could we ever be okay with it?

The moment we think that something will last for ever, we begin to fear the loss of it and we expose ourselves to experiencing it. But what if the end is actually the beginning of everything and every separation is really a reunion with ourselves?

Rewrite Your Patterns

Write down a list of the most important romantic relationships in your life. Next to each name write:
1. What do/did I like about this person?

2. What do/did I dislike about him/her?

3. What triggered me the most in this person?

Now, after making a detailed list for every individual, reflect on what you've written. What do they all have in common; what are the common triggers? Is there anything that triggers you repeatedly, in the same areas? What was the common accusation you made towards all of them? For example, you might realise: *In all my relationships I was triggered by my partner not knowing how to express his love to me or not making me feel loved enough. They were all emotionally unavailable.*

Now ask yourself, is this the absolute truth? Can you find at least three examples to contradict your accusation? Ask yourself: Is it possible that what I was accusing them of was something I was performing myself? For example: *Did I know how to express my love to them, did I make them feel loved? Was I emotionally available?*

Find the patterns that keep repeating themselves in your life and free yourself from them and you will never attract similar situations or people ever again.

12

Self-Fulfilment

We should not enter any relationship in deficiency,
but rather a full tank, ready for a long drive.

•

Can you recognise your needs?
Can you acknowledge your needs?
Can you accept your needs?
Can you honour your needs?
Can you communicate your needs?
Can you fulfil your needs?

Often the first thing we complain about in our relationship is that our needs are not fulfilled. Why is that? Because relationships are there to show us what needs we are not fulfilling for ourselves. What do you think the other person can give you that you can't give to yourself?

For many years, I was not able to identify what were my needs. And even those I was aware of I would either ignore or discount. My own insecurity would make me settle for second best. I would ignore what was truly important for me, just to receive anything. I started to ignore my own needs and longings.

Today, I know that I am creating everything in my life and everything comes from me.

I see every experience as a gift because that helps me to discover more truth about myself. When I feel ignored by people and I get triggered, I ask: What am I ignoring in myself? When

I feel I'm not receiving enough attention, I ask: Where am I not giving enough attention to myself? When I am rejected, I ask: What parts of myself am I rejecting?

Triggers are nothing but a warm light shining on our own unhealed scars. The pain they cause us is our own pain that we have created. We are never really angry with other people for causing us suffering; we are angry with ourselves for creating that suffering for ourselves by ignoring what is important to us. On a deep level, we do know and feel that every experience in this life comes from us.

We create for ourselves messages and signs to guide ourselves towards higher alignment with our soul. This reality, your life, shows you who you are in the external world. Mixes of different people, places and experiences create a cocktail of who you are. As you evolve, those people, places and experiences change.

So to change anything in your life, all you have to do is to look inside yourself and see how you can become the change you want to experience.

A great place to start is with your external world. Whatever is missing in your external world is whatever is missing inside yourself,

What is missing in your world? What is it that you crave, dream about or need? For example: *I would like to receive more appreciation.*

Now, how can you create it for yourself?

First, you need to generate that feeling within yourself for it to manifest externally. Second, you need to start giving what you need to the world around you. Third, you need to start communicating what you need to the world around you. Fourth, you need to stop settling for anything less than what you truly desire.

Ask yourself:

- If I would like to receive more appreciation, how can I create it myself? How much do I see and acknowledge everything I am good at and everything I am contributing? Do I give myself the recognition I expect from others?
- Do I give to others what I want to receive myself? Am I able to share compliments, recognise others' efforts and acknowledge their gestures, commitments or contribution?
- Do I see and appreciate people for what and who they are and what they offer?
- Do I communicate to others, openly and lovingly, my need for appreciation? Am I able to ask for it or do I expect the other person to read my mind? Can I ask, for example: *I worked very hard on this project, would you have any positive feedback to share to encourage me to invest myself further?* Or can I ask a friend: *What do you like about me?*
- If I have put a serious effort into something and given my absolute best and someone is not giving me what I have asked for or what I choose to experience, am I able to communicate with love that I will invest my time differently as I choose, and not settle for anything less than the best experience I can create?

In my experience, if you focus on the first and second part, the third and fourth won't even be needed. You will create in your experience with others exactly what you are with yourself. What influences how we feel about other people is simply how we feel about ourselves.

Every need we have works similarly. It asks for our attention first. It asks to not be ignored or pushed away. It asks to be recognised, accepted and fulfilled – by ourselves first.

We only ignore our own needs when we don't believe that we can fulfil them ourselves, when we don't trust our own power of creation and when we forget that we are the source of everything and everything comes from us.

Sometimes our needs have nothing to do with other people, but are simply about time and space for ourselves.

To Do List

Many of us are overwhelmed with different daily tasks. We have our lists of 'things to do' and then more lists, of things that we will do once all those tasks are ticked. Right?

But, somehow that first list seems to never end. We keep hoping things will change and we will finally get some more time for ourselves. But does it ever happen?

Will the world ever stop running so fast? Hmm, what do you think?

In the past, I would try to get to the end of the list as fast as possible and would be so exhausted at the end of it that those few moments of free time I did get before the next task's storm would just be recovery time.

I realised that those peaceful free moments were eluding me more and more. I had to learn to redesign my days, to categorise my tasks, to prioritise what is truly important, but most of all, to discover what actually fills my cup and what is emptying it.

What Fills and Empties Your Cup?

It is simple. Think about what tasks or activities boost your energy and lift you up and what drains your energy.

Never focus only on those second ones, otherwise, you will burn out very quickly. Keep a balance; start your week, and ideally your day, with purpose, by doing things that energise you. You will see a massive change in how you feel and how your work feels. You will be more rested, satisfied and most of all inspired. You will no longer wait for things to change, you will be your own change.

I used to wait until I had finished all my 'have to do' tasks before I started to do the fun, creative, inspiring things. Now, I do the fun bits first in order to have enough energy to do my 'have to do' tasks.

Don't wait to finish everything you have to
do before you start doing what you truly love.
Start doing what you truly love and use
that inspiration and energy to do all the rest.
Stop ignoring yourself and you will
never be ignored by others.

Needs Check-in

We should not enter any relationship with a deficiency but rather with a full tank, ready to drive us on.

Sit comfortably in a quiet place, take your journal and ask yourself: What do I crave the most in my relationship with other people at the moment? How do I ask them to be with me? What do I ask them to give me? What do I want to receive from them? Be as specific as possible. Write down at least three different things.

For example: I expect my partner to spend more quality time with me.

Then reflect on the feelings connected to this statement. That might be: I expect my partner to spend more quality time with me because quality time makes me feel connected with him.

Now ask yourself: Do I give myself enough of that feeling? Do I spend enough quality time with myself? What does connecting to myself look like? What does it mean to me?

Then write on another sheet of paper what it is that you get the most upset about in your relationships with other people right now.

For example:

I get upset when someone ignores me. When they don't show me empathy.

Ask yourself: How have I been ignoring myself? What are the needs that I have been ignoring? When have I been too hard on myself?

It is great to check in with yourself, as often as possible, but ideally once a month. Check where you are at. What are your needs that you might be ignoring and how can you fulfil them? When you fulfil your needs you will be fulfilled by life in general.

Stillness

For the next thirty days do not use your phone for the first thirty minutes after you wake up. Don't switch it on! In that thirty minutes, find at least fifteen minutes to sit quietly doing nothing. No television, no book, no journaling. Simply be with yourself in silence. Let ideas come to you. If your mind is not quiet, focus on everything that you love in your life. Feel the gratitude filling you up.

13

Self-Suggestion

In a game, when you master a certain skill,
a new game level opens up. In life,
when you reach a certain level of awareness,
a new reality opens up.

•

When you stop telling yourself one story, another emerges.

People rarely ask: '*What can I learn about myself through this experience?*' but rather '*What can this experience give me?*' or '*How can this person make me happier?*'

The questions we ask are important. They show us what we focus on. What we focus on is what we feel. What we feel defines the way we experience life. So, what questions do you ask? We cannot stop the process of thinking but we can decide the quality of our thoughts. We can choose to pose ourselves positive or negative questions. If you had the chance to get the answer to any question you could pose, what would you like to know? Would you ask: *Why don't I get along with my partner? Why can't I find love? Why am I alone? Why am I unhappy? What is wrong with me?*

Or, would you rather ask: *How can I experience love? What can I do to attract a soulmate? How can I be happier? Am I with the right person? If I am with the right person, what can I do to make the relationship better? What is great about me?*

Can you see the difference? The first set of questions always implies negative answers. Answers like, you are alone because you are blocked, you emit bad energy or you simply do nothing to meet someone.'

Negative answers will bring negative feelings, which in turn will bring about even more negative energy. Life always gives true answers to your questions. Therefore, if you ask why you are unhappy, you will find out. The universe will show you, precisely, the origins of your bad mood. If you instead ask about how you can become joyful, therefore, you will receive the necessary guidelines and tools to experience happiness and joy.

How Do You Choose to Experience Yourself?

I believe that where we put our attention we put our energy. Words create thoughts and feelings. Both thoughts and feelings generate vibrations that create our reality. Usually, the thought comes first, then the feeling follows. Sometimes, it's the other way round. However, we cannot feel and think at the same time. So when I ponder on what consciousness is, I stop being conscious. When I reflect upon love, I stop feeling it. When I wonder where I would like to be, I am not here and now any more.

Many people don't know how to change their feelings at will. Some of us don't know how to change our thoughts. But all of us know how to change our words. Let's then start there.

Marilyn Jenett in her book *Feel Free to Prosper* says that if we keep repeating certain words the things they represent will materialise in our life.[22] So someone who often uses words like doubt, stress, uncertain, problem, lack, bad or little will experience the manifestation of those words. And in order to manifest our desires, the conscious and subconscious minds must agree; so even if we try to be positive by saying, for example, *it no longer irritates* me, our subconscious mind still hears the negative word 'irritates', which is the dominant word in the sentence. So it thinks we want to be irritated. It is much more powerful to just eliminate negative words entirely and say instead: *I started to enjoy it*, for example. Or simply: *I am okay with it*. We have to learn to monitor our language and eliminate every word that is negative. Use words you would like to see manifesting in your life, speak about things you would like to experience and talk yourself into a new way of being. The rest will follow.

The Marriage of Conscious and Subconscious Mind

This marriage creates magic; when both minds have agreed on the idea, that idea will manifest. But when the conscious mind embeds an idea in the subconscious mind, the subconscious mind has first to accept it, which it can only do when there is no confusion or contradictory messages. Once we do plant the seed, and nurture it with positive thoughts and expectations, then we turn the job over to a universal mind and we can let go.

Canadian writer Brian Tracy stresses the importance of writing down our objectives on paper.[23] It helps to clarify them, but most of all it drives them into our subconscious, which will lead us towards them in life. Writing down objectives and deadlines for achieving them is often a required task for MBA students. Therefore, it is important to be particularly careful with what we write, say, predict or assume.

I used to be really afraid of flying. My aviophobia manifested after my first flying experience and got so out of control that I would have to either take sedatives or cancel my trip. I had no idea what to do. I knew I wanted to travel and to get to some places the train was not an option.

So one day I decided that I was going to fall in love with flying. I would go to the airport and make my experience there as enjoyable as possible. Good coffee, my favourite music in my headphones, amazing books... anything and everything that I was in love with, to create a positive association with flying. I repeated to myself as often as possible: I fall in love with flying more and more.

After a few months I completely forgot that I had ever had a flying problem. I truly fell in love with flying. Through creating my own positive association with it I had ordered my unconsciousness to love it. Now I have travelled to over fifty countries, have lived in over ten and have travelled as a location-independent entrepreneur for many years taking a plane sometimes more then forty times a year.

Joseph Murphy in his book *The Power of Your Subconscious Mind*, writes about the importance of words and thoughts in our life, how important it is to always think and speak positively, yet without lying to ourselves.[24] Therefore, if we are ill and tell ourselves that we are healthy, our subconscious minds know that is a lie. Then we become even more frustrated, which gives us the opposite result to what we want. It is much better to use expressions that are not so contradictory. For example: 'I am in the process of recovery; I am getting better with every day; I feel better with every moment.' The subconscious mind knows these are not lies, so it treats these thoughts as an order to act.

Our Thoughts Create Our Reality

If I am not able to keep myself from sharing my negative thoughts with others, I try at least to be very mindful of what

I verbalise. I always try to employ the past tense ('I was not feeling happy today because...') or end with a positive hint ('I believe my situation is already changing for the better'). Notice that even if I speak about being sad I still use the word happy, as our subconscious mind hears and focuses on dominant words.

According to André Charbonnier, complaining and thinking negatively about our problems, although it may bring temporary relief, does not free us from them.[25] In fact the reverse is true; energy flows to the place we focus on, so the more energy we put into negative thoughts and words, the bigger our problems will be. That's why it is wise to focus on exchanging our negative thoughts for positive ones. As soon as we recognise a negative thought, we should immediately turn instead toward optimism:

- It's going to get better.
- With every moment, my situation is improving.
- Everything is falling into place.
- I know it is going to be alright.
- I believe I will find a positive solution.
- This situation is for my own good.

If we have been thinking negatively for a long time, our body will have been conditioned to feel bad. If our body feels bad, we will generate even more negative thoughts as we try to find a source for our feelings. But the truth is that sometimes we simply are in a low mood and there is no real external reason for it.

The only way to break this cycle is to not feed those feelings with negative thoughts. By controlling our thoughts, with a bit of practice we can create the state of mind we desire.

If you do wake up in a bad mood, simply be gentle with yourself. Do things unusually. Try to do a bit less than you had planned and do something for yourself instead.

Don't complain, don't criticise your life, yourself or those around you.

Don't be too hard on yourself – and most of all, don't take any important decisions today. Try to take care of yourself the way you would take care of your best friend. Do something you like: read a book, watch a comedy. Before you realise it, the feeling will be gone. It is only what we resist that persists.

Most of us have been taught to think negatively since early childhood. You might remember your parents saying things like, 'Don't climb that tree, you'll fall!' Unfortunately, the process of socialisation often deprives us of the great possibilities we started life with. If we keep repeating the same action or reaction, it will become automatic; recorded in the mind as an answer to a situation or behaviour and used subconsciously so that we start to respond to things on autopilot.

The only way to change these patterns is to create new thoughts and to question absolutely everything. We walk around making the same mistakes, meeting the same problems, creating the same kind of energy – until we understand what we must change. The same thoughts produce the same feelings, and the same feelings produce the same thoughts. If we stay in the same way of thinking, and in the same feelings, we generate the same energy, which creates the same reality.

Thoughts, feelings, words and actions have creative power. What we think influences the events in our life. What we think influences what we feel. Words follow thoughts, then we act. When we say what we think, we enhance the energy of the thoughts that are sent into the universe. That energy, as we have seen, attracts like energy. Nothing can change unless we break our pattern.

And it is enough to change our thoughts. We do not have to change the entire world around us to see changes around us. So, let us give our perception a chance to unleash the magnificent creative energies we have within. It is we who are the lords of our fate.

The power of our beliefs

'According to your faith, it is done to you,' says the Bible. We all hear stories about the power of faith and belief, especially when it comes to miracles of healing physical conditions. The placebo effect is as old as medicine, but now we have scientific evidence to indicate that under the right circumstances, a placebo can be just as effective as traditional treatments. 'The placebo effect is more than positive thinking – believing a treatment or procedure will work. It's about creating a stronger connection between the brain and body and how they work together,' says Professor Ted Kaptchuk of Harvard-affiliated Beth Israel Deaconess Medical Center, whose research focuses on the placebo effect.[26] Our minds can be a powerful healing tool when given the chance.

On the other hand, if we believe that a black cat crossing our path brings us bad luck, and we see one doing that, we might panic and attract all sorts of negative scenarios that day, for which we will blame the poor cat. Things like tribal curses work similarly; they use self-suggestion and hetero-suggestion. If you believe that you are not very lucky or that your situation can't get any better, it probably won't.

Joseph Murphy has a well-known saying: 'When something comes down, the rest will follow.'[27] Have you ever noticed that when something goes wrong in your life, suddenly everything starts to go wrong? Why is that so? Murphy says that it's not due to bad luck. It's due to the fact that at the moment of that negative event, we create huge deposits of negative energy, which are then sent into the universe and attract even more negative energy and unfavourable events. And things start to spiral.[28] All of a sudden, we might lose our job, we might have a fight with our lover, we might lose our wallet or our car might break down. Murphy explains that people might think inwardly that the situation cannot get worse, but because we have reacted negatively to one adverse event, a series of misfortunes will follow. Your reality is the evidence of your thoughts and beliefs. What we define as negative is always a result of something or a source of it. If we found the cause or waited for the result before judging something to be 'good' or 'bad', we would avoid putting ourselves through the stress of the situation. Everything can be perceived as a problem or as a chance. Sometimes situations that seem bad can be our deliverance, and can lead us to fulfil our dreams.

Positive Thinking

The human mind is not able to think about positive and negative things simultaneously, so we need to choose. Remember: our perception creates our reality; we can choose whether we focus on the glass being half-full or half-empty.

We cannot think and feel at the same time and we cannot think about two things at the same time. If we concentrate on carnal sensation, we will stop thinking. If we focus on visual perception, we stop thinking. Similarly, when we concentrate on something positive, bad thoughts go away. We cannot stop the activity of the mind, yet we can choose the kind of thinking it's involved in. There are two ways of living. Inside your mind or outside of it. Only one of them can ever make you feel alive.

Activating positive energy

One of my favourite methods for doing this, which I use very often, is visualisation. I recall positive memories. I feed my mind by thinking about moments that evoke joy. I often also say positive mantras out loud, or write them down on a sheet of paper and keep rewriting them every day for a period of time. I often use them as my computer or phone screensaver – anywhere where I will see them the most often.

My favourite mantra for years has been: *Everything is perfect.* I say it every single time any challenging situation appears. And guess what? It always turns out to be perfect for me. When I do this I always focus on how I would like to feel today. When our perception changes, the whole world around transforms. In a game, when you master a certain skill, a new game level opens up. In life, when you reach a certain level of awareness, a new reality opens up.

We start meeting different people, get new job opportunities, get invited to have new experiences or change the character of our current relationships. Whatever happens it will be a whole new life waiting for you.

Self-Description

Ask yourself: What kind of words do I use to describe myself to other people? Are those words positive or negative? How am I creating myself?

Programme Your Reality

Create your own mantras to repeat to yourself as much and as often as possible. Some examples are below:

- My life is becoming better in every aspect.
- Every situation serves me well.
- Every day I attract gorgeous people and situations.
- Day by day I become more happy and contented with life.
- Day by day I love myself more and I trust myself more.
- Everything happens from me.

14

Self-Validation

Sometimes accepting that you are NOT good enough
is a bigger step towards self-love than trying
to constantly prove otherwise.

•

It is never the external things that add to our value,
but our acting out of fear that diminishes it.

How much do you think you are worth?

Every one of us measures our own value in many different
ways: how many projects we have completed, the number of social
media followers we have gained, how many hours we have spent
in the gym, the figure on our bank account balance, how many
people have loved us or how many people we have made smile.

Our self-worth can grow or shrink depending on how we measure it and what is important to us. The interesting thing is that all of
these measurements have nothing really to do with our true value.

What if all the things you have in your life were suddenly
taken from you? Would your self-worth stay the same? It
probably wouldn't. You might feel less than before. Why? No
one has taken anything from who you are. So would you agree
that we have given external things the power to take our self-
worth from us?

You are born perfect. You have unlimited access to love, security, self-worth, self-confidence. You have an amazing abundance
of self-fulfilment. You don't have to own anything to feel joyful,

happy and worthy. It is later on, when you are taught the value of external things, that you start to compare that value to yourself.

The secret is that external, material things have very different values from the value we are born with. Not comparable. It doesn't matter how many things you own or don't, your value does not change. Your account balance might change, or the house you live in, but that will never change how worthy you are as a person. When you compare two children to each other, one from a very wealthy family and another from a very poor one, one very good at maths, the other very good at sports, do you measure them differently? Do you feel one of them is worth more than the other just because their situation is different? Not really.

Every and each one of us is unique and different. There is no other person like you in this world, with your gifts, your smile, your abilities and your experiences. We are none of us comparable to anyone else. So every one of us must be perfect exactly the way we are.

Self-Validation and Security

Imagine you had 100 per cent confidence and self-worth. How differently would you react to situations and events in your life?

Imagine that, after your first date together, someone never calls you. If this is a measurement of how worthy you feel about yourself, you will instantly feel triggered and rejected. You might blame yourself, try to figure out what you have done wrong, or simply search for the reasons for their behaviour in yourself.

If, however, you feel secure with who you are, you will simply either call them first to check in and ask what happened or accept that they are not available and are not looking for the same things as you. You are grateful that you didn't waste your time and that you found out early on that they weren't the right match for you.

Most of our behaviour arises out of insecurity. When we are insecure, other people's actions towards us become a way for us to value ourselves rather than just information about them and only them.

**You can't choose how people will act,
you can only choose how you react.**

If someone doesn't call you when you wanted them to or thought they would, what does it say about you? Nothing. What does it say about them? They might be busy, they might not need regular contact, they might not feel like speaking to you or maybe even they are not that interested in you. Even these last two are only about them; they have nothing to do with how worthy you are. Do you like everyone in your life? No. So don't expect everyone will always like you.

When you feel worthy within yourself you will never create situations in your life that make you feel insecure or unworthy. When you feel unworthy, though, you will look for proof of your unworthiness everywhere to show to yourself that you are right. You will interpret insignificant events as being deliberate actions against you. And you will suffer.

Our suffering does not really come from someone doing something wrong to us; it comes mainly from our interpretation of this situation and the blame for it we try to find in ourselves.

If your biggest fear is being rejected, for example, as mine was, you will see rejection everywhere, in other people's every small action or behaviour, and you might blame yourself for it or feel like a victim, which will take away your sense of security. But punishing yourself for causing the situation, rather than giving yourself credit for creating it, is simply a choice. When you want someone to do something for you, you don't really crave that specific gesture, but the feeling this action will create in you. The feeling of appreciation, recognition, attention or love. If the person you expected to call you HAD called you as you wanted them to, you would feel safe and secure. Did you really need to talk to them about something, did you really want to see them again, were you that interested? Maybe not. But you wanted to feel safe from being rejected.

If we understand that our state doesn't depend on external forces, that we have all we need within ourselves to feel secure, then we need never feel insecure or unworthy again.

You can choose to believe that external forces validate you, or you can choose not to.

Act Worthy and Secure

If you are not sure how to react to something, ask yourself, 'How would a completely secure person behave in this situation? If I knew that my worth didn't depend on any outside situation, how would I act right now?'

Think about someone who you consider to be worthy and secure. How would they act? Or how would you act in the company of someone who you feel secure and worthy with?

When we feel unworthy or insecure, whatever we do, we simply act from fear. And when we act from fear we will always attract precisely what we fear. Whatever we do from love will bring us nothing but love, trust and confidence. Whatever we do from fear will bring us misalignment, confusion, insecurity and self-doubt. It is never the external things that add to our value, but our acting out of fear that diminishes it.

Self-confidence doesn't come from gaining
more knowledge, more wealth and more personality, but
from giving up the fear of not knowing,
not having and not being perfect.

Break free, today, from acting out of your fears. Start small, think secure and worthy, and act accordingly.

Letter to Yourself

Write a letter to yourself from your future self. What would you tell yourself now if you were ten years older, wiser and more confident? What advice would you give yourself? What would you ask yourself to care about, and what would you ask yourself to let go of? How would you ask yourself to be with yourself and others? Write down everything that you think your younger self might want to hear from your older, reassuring self.

15

Who Do You Fight With?

Often when we see the best in people,
people become their best.

•

Every fight is an inner fight.

•

Each expectation we create in external
reality comes from the shortage
we have created within ourselves.

Why do we fight with the people we love the most? Because the very thing we're in conflict over is the same thing that attracted us to our partner, as Esther Perel says.[29] Every person who comes into the world fights for their basic needs. Regardless of sex/gender, we all need security, reliability, predictability, affiliation and continuity. But all of us also need adventure, development, mystery, risk, discovery and exploration. We must balance these needs for security and adventure, unity and autonomy, oneness and freedom, love and desire. Many of us find partners whose strengths mirror our flaws (whether these flaws are true or just in our minds) because we imagine we need to make up for our shortcomings in those areas. But according to Esther Perel, need is the greatest 'anti-aphrodisiac'.[30]

Arguing with Ourselves

Quarrels are a desperate request for love, approached indirectly. Everything we do comes either from love or from a cry for love. Sometimes we provoke a fight, make a scene, threaten our partner with a break-up, to get the evidence of love, to test their love to be sure they won't leave us. To feel that our partner still loves us and to prove to ourselves that we still love them as well. There is no better way to appreciate what we have than feeling the fear of losing it.

Relationships are the quickest way to work on ourselves, because they make us confront ourselves. Arguments show the truth about ourselves; they show us our reflection in the mirror. Our partner's so-called flaws that we complain about are, in most cases, our own shadows (remember the shadow from earlier in the book?), which we do not wish to look at. They invite us to introduce changes into our lives and encourage us into contemplation; they motivate us to work on ourselves. And most of all, arguments teach us to address our own needs.

Everything that triggers us and provokes us into starting an argument or a conflict comes in fact from within ourselves. Being triggered means there is a past event within you that hasn't been fully resolved or accepted. And that trigger is giving you a beautiful gift – it is pointing at that part of yourself that you have maybe buried, ignored or never expressed.

Until those parts are voiced, you will create in your life situations and events that will trigger the same feelings over and over. You will attract similar people, situations or events that are there to try to show yourself what you are afraid to look at or to hear.

So if someone is ignoring you, most likely you are ignoring certain parts of yourself. If someone doesn't give you the attention you desire, most likely you can't give this attention to yourself either.

Every trigger is a gift because it is an opportunity to see something that screams for your attention. The more you fight that process, the more you will find yourself fighting not only with other people but – most importantly – with yourself. If you're aware that you're fighting with your partner or someone else a lot, ask yourself about a few fundamental things:

- Have you been listening to your inner voice or have you been ignoring it?
- Have you been honouring your own needs or have you been compromising them?
- Have you been giving to yourself enough attention and care or have you been expecting others to provide it for you?

Every fight is an inner fight. We have been fighting our own desires, our dreams, our ideas, our needs. We have been compromising our true longings and by doing so creating misalignment with who we truly are.

**And if we are not aligned with ourselves,
we will experience in external reality discordant,
inharmonious events and experiences
that mirror our inner state.**

We can't ever feel overwhelmed by our own emotions if we stay centred. When we are aligned with ourselves, even if bad things happen to us we receive them with acceptance, because we know that we have been truthful to ourselves all along.

Anything that we do, we do either from our heart or our mind. It is when those two start to fight with each other that we feel doubts, we seek other people's opinions, we don't know what to do. It is a very uncomfortable process. We only seek the

opinion of other people to convince ourselves that we are right –
but if we have sought that opinion in the first place, it means that
we are probably not! It means that whatever was done probably
came from our mind rather than our heart; when we do things
from our heart, there is no hesitation, doubt or uncertainty. Only
a relief, acceptance and a sense of peace. That I promise.

Mind

Our thoughts are not who we truly are; they are just a projection
of our mind. Our mind doesn't want what is best for us. It
plays games, it judges, it doubts, it catastrophises, it panics,
it exaggerates, it confuses us, it criticises us, it changes its
opinion and it scares us. This is why 'mindfulness' practices like
meditation emphasise getting out of our thoughts; changing
our perception and refocusing on what is: our body, the place
around us, our breath, the beat of our heart.

Decisions taken with our heart bring instantaneous relief.
The thoughts will still question that decision, because that is
what the mind does; but when they do, we won't feel bad about
it any more and we will be able to let go of them easily. The
role of our mind is to question, to doubt, to fight. Our role is
to understand that our thoughts are just an illusion of who we
think we are. If we can observe our thoughts, it simply means we
must be something else.

If we learn how to listen to the inner voice of our heart and
to follow it, we will never find ourselves in misalignment, either
with ourselves or with other people. There won't be any reason for
arguments or disagreements. We will feel lightness in our heart.

The heart doesn't question because the heart is never afraid.
Love can't be afraid because love is the very opposite of fear. The

heart doesn't adhere to any rules but the 'rule' of what is right for you in this moment. And when you do what is right for you it will always be right for other people too. It will always contribute to their growth in one way or another. And you will be peaceful about it.

If you start to feel uncomfortable, sad or frustrated at any point, simply sit down and listen. Your mind might start to blame the situation around you or your partner for your frustrations, as it is trying to quickly fix it. But the real reason is always hidden somewhere deeper within ourselves. Reflect: where is the misalignment coming from? What is your heart telling you to do that you are not doing? What needs are you ignoring?

Maybe you are supposed to do something, take an action, speak to someone, let go of something or take a break. The more you push it away, the more discomfort you will feel and the more you will project your frustration onto others, causing conflicts and disconnection.

When you follow your gut you will very quickly realise that not only does it bring you instant relief and joy but that it also might create some miraculous opportunities in your life. Your intuition works through your desires. Maybe you feel like having a break from work and going for a walk but your mind is telling you that it is not a good idea because you have too much work that you must finish. You can ignore your desire, get frustrated and perhaps even react by taking it out on your colleagues. Or you can choose to honour your desire and go for a walk anyway. Now, maybe on the walk, you will meet the very love of your life, or an old friend who is looking for a business partner; or you may simply recharge your energy level so you can experience new inspirations and ideas. You never know. If, however, you just stay and work, the chances that you will do your best possible work are very low because, simply, your heart is not in it. Your heart wants you to do something else that is the best thing you can do in that specific moment. Trust it. Learn how to trust your heart and your heart will guide you, away from any conflicts, frustrations and fights.

If you don't know how to follow your heart, simply ask yourself: What would love do?

Again, everything can be perceived as a problem or as a chance. Sometimes situations that seem bad lead us to simply fulfil our dreams.

Letting go is the most beautiful art we can practise. Letting go means to stop holding on to something: an idea, a belief, an emotion, a thought. Anything that we hold on to too tightly stops us from receiving something else, it stops us from seeing anything else and sometimes it stops us from moving forward.

How to Let Go and Not Argue?

Every time we expect something from someone we expose ourself to being disappointed. Every time we demand that someone do something for us, we are in the dynamic of trying to control them. And every time we want someone to be a certain way, we condition our love for them.

It is important to communicate our desires but never from a place of neediness, expectation or lack of acceptance. Why? Because the person will feel that we love them only conditionally and will simply do the opposite of what we desire. Our demand will make the person feel unmotivated, rejected and unaccepted, and criticised for how they are. When we expect something from someone we assume that we are right. But there is no right or wrong, there is only what is right for individuals.

The first step in asking for what you want is to let go of your expectation. Every time you feel frustrated with someone or you expect something, ask yourself: *What do I want from this person? Why do I think that this person has to give it to me? Can I instead give it to myself?* And let go.

Once you have let go, you are ready to ask for what you want from a place of love. When you ask someone to do something from this place of love, you make them feel important, needed and helpful. And this is the best motivator you can ever create.

So: Imagine you are making dinner and you would like your partner to help you. Asking from a place of expectation would sound something like: *You never help me when I cook for us. Can you do something instead of just sitting there reading?*

Asking for help from a loving place would sound something like: *Perhaps you are busy right now but I would love you to help me to chop these onions.*

You can see the difference. If you are not sure how to ask for something, ask yourself: how would I like to be asked? Every time you notice neediness inside you – let go of it. Every time you ask someone to do something – ask with love.

16

Reunite All Sides of Yourself

Your strength doesn't come from raising rocks
and building walls around yourself, it comes
from the ability to rise beyond the
walls and rocks that have been limiting
your truest expression.

•

If someone rejects you for who you truly are, it's only
because they are afraid to face all parts of themselves.

At different times all of us show different sides of ourselves, different facets and different alter egos created to act and perform in different circumstances and situations. Some of these sides have been developed as a protective or objective-driven mechanism, others we were born with and they exist within us so we can experience all sides of ourselves, and experience ourselves as everything. They exist as very opposite energies that can fight with each other, seek domination or hide behind our preferred facets, influencing our thoughts and actions.

Every side is activated by what stands in front of us. A challenge, an experience, a person. Every person activates different sides of us, depending on what is active in them. That's why we act, feel and behave slightly differently with different people and that's why sometimes we want to see one person and not another, depending what we desire to express within ourselves.

Every person has their own individual sides of themselves, unique to who they are; but we all, regardless of our sex or gender, carry two main polarities within ourselves – our feminine and our masculine energy – and can and must embody both. Those qualities have often been very stereotypically boxed and framed, and can stop us discovering our individual expression of them. Because society generally encourages us to embody masculine energy, we have all subconsciously started to discriminate against our feminine side, often completely disconnecting from it. Many of us have embodied masculine, goal-driven postures to succeed in the world. We have focused on doing rather than being, thinking rather than feeling and getting rather than receiving.

What are thought of as masculine qualities – independence, strength, leadership, power – are often considered more attractive, desired and cherished; by contrast, traditional feminine qualities – like nurturance, sensitivity, empathy, expressiveness – are often viewed as weakness. How many of us have become driven towards gaining, dominating, controlling, succeeding or achieving rather than allowing, surrendering, trusting, expressing and creating?

But if we are not aligned with all the elements of who we are, we can only ever succeed as someone who we are not. And can succeeding as someone we are not really ever bring us joy and fulfilment?

When as a society we hear so many phrases and ideas like 'Man up', we can start to hide our other opposing qualities; suppress them, be ashamed of them and reject them. This creates an inner fight that can easily become a source of conflicts in both our inner and our outer world.

Being asked to be more manly or womanly puts us under pressure to follow a stereotype – we are boxed in by an idea and concept that is far from our individual expression of masculinity or femininity.

The interesting question about 'manly' or 'womanly' qualities is what they could mean to you.

I believe that there is nothing more courageous than being vulnerable.

I believe that there is nothing more powerful than knowing how to trust.

I believe that there is nothing more brave than showing our feelings.

But what is important is what this idea means to you and how you choose to express all sides of yourself regardless of what others think. However your individual expression looks, express yourself fully. Both polarities create the beauty of who you are and how you are.

Become Whole

Your strength doesn't come from collecting the rocks and building walls around yourself, it comes from the ability to rise beyond the walls and rocks that have been limiting your truest expression. Your strength comes from reuniting all the parts of yourself and becoming a whole. It comes from standing up for who you are and what you feel at every given moment. It comes from the courage to own and show every aspect of yourself fully.

We are not going to witness the true power and strength of a person if we devalue the side traditionally thought of as feminine: the very side that includes the qualities of gentleness, vulnerability, empathy, humility, sensitivity and intuition. The very side that we often crave to experience in another person but at the same time somehow discourage them from embodying. Maybe this is because we, ourselves, are so afraid to embody this side fully. Conditioned to act and behave as strong, independent and unbreakable, we don't even realise that we, too, have lost touch with our soft, sensitive, vulnerable side.

What the world needs the most is for all of us to embody those parts of ourselves that have been rejected or considered weak. Giving someone space to embrace all parts of themself and to discover their full potential requires that we do the same for ourselves. That can be scary.

Let the other person show you who they are by letting them discover themselves. Let's stop desiring to be someone's weakness and choose to support their true strength! It's time we started seeing people for what they are beyond the expectations placed on them by their sex or gender. It's time to set each other free. The same polarity that needs to exist between two people in order to create an attraction and desire needs to also exist in balance inside of each of us, to create an alignment within and deepen our connection with ourselves and other people.

What Happens When We Are Unbalanced?

When we spend too much time dominating or controlling and we forget to surrender, we become drained, unmotivated, burned-out, depressed and overwhelmed. We simply don't have the energy to move forward any more. We have used up our whole stock of energy and haven't recharged ourselves. We must remember that every movement requires stillness, every action requires inaction, every domination requires submission, every control requires surrender, every creation requires undoing and every knowing requires unknowing and trust. It's time to stop, to breathe and restore. If you feel drained, overwhelmed and lost, these are not signs that something must be done so much as a sign that something must be received. When you don't feel that you can hold yourself, you must surrender and allow the universe to hold you instead. If on the other side we have been only nourishing ourselves without taking any action in our life, we have stopped creating. We need the dance of both polarities in our life in order to stay in balance and to use all the gifts and potential that are hidden within us.

Vulnerability Task

Sit in a quiet place and reflect on how you feel about yourself when you are with other people. Do you feel weak, intimidated or uncomfortable, or do you feel liberated, empowered and truthful? What were the expectations that your parents or parental figures put on you? Did they expect you to be strong at all times and not to cry, or did they allow you to show your emotions? Or perhaps they treated you as weak, helping you with everything? Reflect on how they behaved themselves? Were they open with what they were feeling or rather closed, hiding their inner experiences? When upset, did they shut down and withdraw, or communicate their needs and feelings? Did you perceive them as weak or strong or perhaps as balanced? Do you see yourself in your parental figures?

Write on a sheet of paper what observations you have about both your parents, or other parental figures in your life.

Are these observations the ones that you can recognise in yourself? How differently do you choose to act, now, when you can see more clearly what has been conditioning you?

This week, be vulnerable with someone in your life. Share something that you have never shared with anyone, or something that is difficult for you to share. Perhaps something you feel weak, guilty or ashamed about. Observe yourself in this process and be proud of yourself for embracing all parts of yourself.

17

Repeating the Same Mistake?

If you build walls around yourself, then anything
coming has to knock many times before you can hear it.

•

We should not be disheartened if the mind fights
against change. We are equipped with everything
we need to heal. All the wisdom and
answers to all the questions are within.

Since we were little we have been learning to become 'somebody'. And the more defined that 'somebody' is, the more secure we feel about ourselves.

This is both good and bad. Security is good. But repeated actions become our habits and then our habits become our character; and our moods transform into a temperament, and then our temperament becomes our personality. And what if our character and personality are not ones that we like?

Rather than allowing our behaviours and feelings to be in constant flux we seem – all of us – to enjoy putting around them a permanent frame that can and does define us, even if this definition is negative.

Why is becoming somebody better than being nobody? Someone who is nobody can become everyone and everything at any given moment. But someone who is somebody has to invest lots of energy in keeping that image up. As Ram Dass says: 'In most of our human relationships, we spend much of our time reassuring one another that our costumes of identity are on straight.'[31]

But who we are and how we behave doesn't only depend on us, but also on the environment and experiences we are exposed to. After we have experienced or have been exposed to the same behaviour or action only once or twice, our mind records the event, then goes on reacting automatically in the same way to similar situations. This is known as schematic thinking, a psychological phenomenon where we make a decision based on prior beliefs about what will or will not work, without taking into account the facts.

When we think schematically, we are, quite often, not conscious of this. This is well illustrated by Pavlov's classic experiment with his dogs – after a few days of the light being switched on just before the dogs were given their food, they started to salivate when they saw just the light, because they associated it with being fed.

Whenever we come across a situation resembling the one from the past, our mind will react as it did before or it might react as it saw someone else reacting. If when you were growing up your family used to react to problems by yelling, you will probably automatically do the same as an adult. This may seem like a negative – and it can cause problems – but having a past does give us a great advantage. It shows us what schematic thinking and behaviours we shouldn't take with us into the future. When we can break free from those patterns we will change our future.

You must be the change you want to see,
for each change starts with you.

If you have the same experiences over and over again, it is because you attract them. If you keep tripping up, it is a sign that you haven't yet found a way around the same obstacle. If you keep having the same bad experiences, it means you are repeating the same behaviours over and over.

How Your Fears Can Materialise

For years I was convinced that people in my life would always reject me in the end, that it was just a matter of time. I developed a kind of complex. Over time, I accepted the situation. I would even announce aloud that inevitably people leave me. And many partners, friends and companions did leave me, often without any reason. They would just disconnect.

One day I went through a painful break-up with a man I was not, if I was being truthful, happy with. Yet, I kept telling myself that this relationship was the best thing that could've happened to me. When we first met, I thought I was in seventh heaven – finally someone loved me! – so I started to cling to him. I held on fast to the relationship and feared losing it. That fear existed only in my head, but I decided to materialise it. I planted that seed. I kept telling people how afraid I was of losing him. I underlined the differences between us instead of focusing on similarities. I kept watering that seed of fear. I discussed my relationship problems with my friends, and with my partner himself.

Finally he came to believe that there was little chance for us to survive and, one day, he said, 'There are so many things that drive us apart.' And, all of a sudden, when I'd least expected it, he left. I was bewildered, heartbroken and shocked – yet, I had foreseen this course of events. I was afraid of it and, what's even worse, I was actually creating it. It took me some time to climb out of that hole and realise what I had really done. With this relationship, life had taught me a lesson and I couldn't come to terms with it. But, for the first time, I started to ask questions. This break-up was so devastating that I couldn't carry on accepting events like it.

But although I somehow knew I had created it, the question was: How and why?

After this intense break-up, for the first time, I looked in the mirror and asked: Is it possible that I have been attracting all these experiences of rejection because I don't think I am loveable? That the very thought that I make people leave me was just attracting more and more experiences of this kind? In a way, I realised, I was punishing myself by undergoing consecutive traumas and ensuring that my beliefs would come true.

But why was I so sure that people would reject me? I asked myself this for the very first time in my life. Because underneath that belief I was holding another belief – that I hurt people. The same way, I thought, as I had hurt my brother. I discovered that all these years I subconsciously believed that it was my fault that my brother felt rejected and less loved and that he suffered. If I hurt people, of course they will reject me; so the only thing I can do to protect both them and myself is to reject them first. Very clever!

I hadn't even realised how much rejection I was creating myself by pushing people away, by not letting anyone in, by never fully opening up, by always being ready for people to leave my life tomorrow. Never getting too attached to anyone or anything. Never needing anyone or anything. Never showing people how much they meant to me. Miss Independent! But who would ever like to be close with someone who never needs them, who never shows their vulnerability or weaknesses in front of them? Who never allows them to be their rock? Who never accepts their help? Who never makes them feel important, valuable and loved? See, I put myself in a victim mentality, thinking everyone rejects me; but it was actually me rejecting everyone.

How to Truly Connect?

I used to think that if I asked for too much or opened up too much, people would push me away. They would see how fragile I was and they would abandon me. But the very opposite was true. The very fact that I was not allowing people to give to me or to take care of me often just gave them the impression that I didn't need or want them. And when someone feels they are not needed – well, they often don't feel like staying. I realised that by being closed and not showing my vulnerability I constantly rejected other people's gifts. I was blocking them from showing their strengths and qualities. I was not allowing them to be greater, stronger, better or more, in order for me to not feel less. But it is in those moments when we show our weaknesses that we can truly connect with another human being. Why? Because it means we let them shine for us.

My being so closed off enabled people only to see the part of me I wanted them to see.

Again, what you do to yourself, people will do back. They will reflect your attitude towards yourself. What you do to other people will also reflect back on how others treat you. So simply how you are and how you behave with yourself or others will become your own experience of life.

That day, I decided to take responsibility for my life. I made up my mind to work on myself. It's not easy to get rid of schematic thinking one has practised one's whole life. And knowing the theory and implementing it are two different things.

It takes both courage and discipline – work, day after day – to put aside old, repeated, negative thoughts in favour of more motivating, positive emotions.

Starting to See

Having decided to change myself, I started to increase my awareness and knowledge. I read many books, learned from many coaches, psychologists, shamans, monks and other spiritual teachers. I studied various disciplines, from positive psychology and the neuroscience of mindfulness to meditation and innovative thinking, in order to understand how I could shift my reality, re-create myself and re-connect – with life, but mostly with myself. I wondered if everything I had learned would work in reality, so I tested it all: I started working with meditation, visualisation, mantras; I used psychological exercises, trainings, technology, plant medicines and many other tools to investigate everything I had been learning about my body and mind.

And I started to see.

So many things became comprehensible, my attitude towards the world changed and I began to appreciate time spent with myself. I learned to love myself. My past experiences stopped influencing me as they used to and I was becoming more and more the person I wanted to be.

One day, I decided I was ready for a new relationship and I started to practise a visualisation, trying to imagine a man I would like to be with. It was not a vision of a man as such but more how I felt in his presence. I imagined him next to me and I tried to feel the love I desired. I was trying to get familiar with the very feeling I would feel being next to him. How would my energy change, how would my world expand? Every time I did normal activities, I would try to bring that energy to my field.

After eleven months of working with all the practices I had been investigating, I went to Australia to visit friends. I could feel a strange energy around me. There are usually great changes after a long period of intensive work on oneself. We are more conscious. Our telepathic properties increase. Intuition and 'reading' of energies become sharper. I knew I was approaching something important. One day when driving I was thinking about my dream relationship. I asked myself a question: When is it going to happen? Then, all of a sudden, a song came on the radio. It had the lyrics, 'Soon, you will meet your love again.' Again? I thought. Have we already met?

A few days later, I went to a bar with my friends. My attention was instantly attracted to a tall handsome man across the room. Our eyes met. Half an hour later, we were talking. The next day, we met again and were talking about our journeys. He asked me what was my favourite place on earth and was happy when I said 'Peru' – it was also his favourite place. We carried on talking – but all of a sudden we both worked out that we had met previously, in Peru, four years before!

What were the chances of us meeting again, after four years, in a random bar on the other side of the world? I thought again of that song I'd heard in the car – 'Soon, you will meet your love again'.

And guess what? He felt exactly how I had visualised it. We started a relationship. For some time we were wildly happy; but after some months my old fears and patterns of thinking started to come out again. I was afraid that he'd leave me, that I'd suffer and fail once more. My fear kept growing and I started to push my partner away. My insecurity created greed for declarations and reassurance. The more I craved to be reassured the less reassured I was getting, as I was assuming that the love was not there.

My fear kept growing and I started to push my partner away. I thought he didn't love me any more and decided I wanted to get out of the relationship. I would tell myself, 'Here I go again, the same old story.'

It was then that I asked myself an important question concerning the trap I had set for myself. I asked myself, 'Who started sending those negative vibrations first? Me or him?' I understood that it was me (Remember, everything starts from ourselves.) So, it was not at all surprising that my partner became distant with me and stopped showing affection; he was responding to my negative perception of our relationship. I would have done the same if I was in his place. It was me who started to project my worries and my fears onto him, pushing him away, not trusting his love and his good intentions. It was me who was becoming cold and distant, trying to protect myself from potential danger created by nothing else but my own fears.

My job was to get out of this trap as soon as possible and be aware enough not to get caught again. That insight was like a cold shower. (By the way, water is perfect as far as cleansing of negative energy is concerned – whenever you feel you might be trapped in some old patterns of thinking, try taking a cold shower. A new perspective might arise). I started to understand that I had a chance not to repeat the same mistakes and not to run away and hide or push someone away, and to believe that everything I choose to create is possible. That if I want a happy relationship based on mutual love, I must focus on such a vision and to act as if that vision was my reality.

I started to visualise the relationship I wanted to build. I began to focus on the feelings of trust, safety, love and harmony. I kept reminding myself to be grateful for the marvellous partner I had met and, even more essentially, I started to believe again that I can create everything I will put my heart into. I trusted that I was in a beautiful, happy relationship, to which fear had no access, and that if something was meant to happen, it simply would.

I underwent positive transformation. Uncertainty abandoned me. Fear dissipated. I could feel my own deep happiness, as well as my partner's.

Two years later it was me who left the relationship. It was a beautiful and inspiring relationship filled with lots of love and trust. But our life missions became very different and we were no longer walking in the same direction. There was not much left to keep us together; our desires became different and we became two different people, growing slowly apart. I knew that in order for us both to evolve I had to follow my own path. This was the biggest proof of self-love I could give to myself. I understood now that I had attracted my partner at a point in my life when fear was still holding me back and that, when I overcame my fear, it was time for him to over-come his. The rejection, which he also feared but had never experienced before, allowed my partner to go within and to open his heart even more. Only a few months later he met his wife. The purpose of the relationship, which was to free ourselves from our limitations, had been achieved. This rela-tionship will always stay in my heart because it gave me an opportunity to stop hiding, break my old thinking, let go of my old beliefs, reprogramme myself and set myself free to show myself, create myself and open up to love. It is not sur-prising that there was so much magic around it.

What Creates Repetitive Events in Our Life?

All the events in our life are in one way or another created by us. But it is not only our thoughts and beliefs that can greatly influence our reality. All the unhealed wounds, traumas and trapped emotions recorded in the memory of our body can manifest as obstructive energy. If they stay stuck in our body and won't get released, they will, with the help of our subconscious, lead to certain encounters and situations coming up over and over again.

For example, we inherit family mysteries – known as The Ancestor Syndrome – which means we unconsciously repeat family errors or traumatic events from previous generations. Anne Ancelin Schützenberger, a French psychologist and psychotherapist, in her book *The Ancestor Syndrome: Transgenerational Psychotherapy and the Hidden Links in the Family Tree,* explains and provides clinical examples of her unique psychogenealogical approach to psychotherapy.[32] She shows how, as mere links in a chain of generations, we may have no choice in having the events and traumas experienced by our ancestors visited upon us in our own lifetime.

Most of our conscious and subconscious beliefs originate in our own childhood, which is when we learned to react to, experience and 'record' reality. The process is similar to recording data; it captures all the traumas from that period, as well as the patterns and values we accept as part of our family and wider society, and they may stay with us throughout our lives.

In a child's world, love and security are fundamental; children experience lack of love and care as a threat to their very existence. Therefore, if the need for love is not met, the child will create in their imagination a fictitious and false picture of reality; if there is no or insufficient love, the child may blame themselves and develop low self-esteem. It is similar with violence and aggression; from the perspective of a child, even these are much better than being ignored, for at least they are receiving attention. The child will assume that there must be reasons for the violent or aggressive behaviour and believe that they earned or deserved it.

These feelings, once recorded, are pushed down into the subconscious mind. Quite often forgotten by the conscious memory, they can still appear in nightmares, a phenomenon defined in psychoanalysis as 'repression'. Repression is a key concept in psychoanalysis, where it is understood as a defence mechanism that 'ensures that what is unacceptable to the conscious mind, and would if recalled arouse anxiety, is prevented from entering into it.'

In adult life, the lie we learned as children constitutes a belief: 'I do not deserve love', 'I'm not worthy of love', 'love hurts', 'It is my fault', 'I am not loveable', 'I am not enough' etc. Such a person will have difficulties building relationships. They will repel love and may well attract either aggressive, withholding, unaffectionate or unavailable partners. Our subconscious mind, in order to preserve the beliefs we created, will 'sabotage' our life according to the programme imprinted in the past.

Ways to Undo Our Patterns

So, the most successful way forward is to understand the emotion and remove the programme. We can change the course of future events in our lives by consciously reprogramming the mind until our subconscious mind adopts the new truth.

Reprogramming is a process requiring great discipline, persistence and, most of all, understanding that the programme does exist and what the reprogramme is. Without knowing the cause of it, however, it is harder to reveal the lie created when we were little and let go of it. Yet, it's possible to look for negative thoughts and replace them with their complete opposites. We should not be disheartened if the mind fights against such a change. It will naturally stick to its old patterns. But the good news is that we are equipped with everything we need to heal our body and mind. All the wisdom and answers to all the questions are within.

Attracting the right things

If we unconsciously attract certain events, we can also consciously attract different ones. It is not the memory from our subconscious mind that recalls the events but the emotion recorded in the body activated by that memory. So to change what we attract we not only have to change our mindset but also understand and realise the unheard emotion trapped inside us.

Let's consider the situations that repeat in your life.

- What emotions are you dealing with when it comes to this situation?
- What are the words that best describe what you are experiencing (or you think you are experiencing)? Are they true?
- How do you feel about this situation?
- How does this situation change you?
- What is this situation preventing you from doing or having, completing, being?
- What bad things could happen if you allowed yourself to achieve this desire?

The answers to these questions can reveal negative emotions that are blocked and harmful beliefs that are stopping you from creating the reality you desire.

When we set our mind to positive thinking, when we are present here and now, many negative emotions will evaporate by themselves. The natural state of our soul is joy, love, peace and happiness, and if we do not feel these things, it means we are not truly ourselves.

Attracting the right people

If we keep attracting the same type of people, we should ask ourselves what type that is; then we can investigate how this type relates to us. If, for example, our partner is greedy, critical, unaffectionate, let's ask if we act the same way towards ourselves.

If we keep attracting the same kind of people and experiences it means we refuse to change ourselves.

Every person is our mirror and we can discover things about ourselves in every person we meet. Therefore, people 'predestined' for us are the ones we are attracting at any given moment. Every person is an answer to where we are at. We can only see part of ourselves; we need others to show us our blind spots. To show us hidden parts of ourselves that keep attracting similar problems and issues. When we re-create ourselves, reprogramme our mind and release the past we can finally create the future we desire, with nothing holding us back.

We can free ourselves from self-created limitations and we can finally start attracting different people, situations and circumstances to our life.

Trigger Release

When you are triggered by a situation in your life, take a moment to reflect before reacting. Sit down with yourself if you can and reflect on it. How triggered are you, from 1 to 10? What triggered you? How did you feel?

For example: 'I am triggered 7 out of 10. I was triggered because that person didn't reply to my message. I felt abandoned and rejected.'

Now, can you remember the first time in your life you felt like this?

'The first time I felt rejected was when my friend in primary school stopped talking to me without any explanation.'

Then ask yourself, what meaning did I give the situation from my past?

'The meaning I gave this situation was that this person didn't like me any more. Therefore, I am not likeable and people will reject me for who I am.'

Now, stand back from this situation and watch it as if it was a movie. See your younger self back at primary school. Picture the behaviour of the other child. See it clearly. Then ask yourself: What possibly could have happened that this child stopped talking to me?

Come up with at least three different possible explanations. For example:

- My friend heard from someone that I'd said something mean about them and felt hurt.
- My friend thought I didn't like him any more.
- My friend was jealous of me.

Now, look at this situation as your older self and try to see how you perceive this situation right now. Do you still see yourself as not likeable? Or can you see that it was the other child who felt triggered and insecure? Can you observe if your perception of this situation is shifting? Do you still feel hurt by this situation?

How do you now perceive your current situation? How triggered are you now from 1 to 10?

Remember, we only feel triggered by current situations when our old wounds from the past are reopened.

The Judgement Mirror

Every time you find yourself judging someone in your mind, say to yourself: *Am I ever like this myself? Do I ever judge it in myself?* Remind yourself that everything you judge in others is really your own reflection on yourself.

18

Self-Trust

Your soul never screams, it whispers.
It doesn't think, it feels.

•

I felt embraced by the arms of the wind and
kissed by the warm rays of the sun.
I wanted to hold the world, but even more,
I wanted the world to hold me.

•

When we trust ourselves and follow our
desires and dreams we set ourselves free to
experience our truest power of creation.
We start creating a reality with unlimited possibilities.

How much do you trust yourself?

We often seek reassurance from other people. Reassurance from our colleagues, from our friends. Confirmation that we are in the right place, confirmation that we are safe and loved. Confirmation that everything will be just fine.

The more appreciation, recognition and reassurance we receive, the better we feel about ourselves. We tend to thrive on riding on a wave of confidence built on this external confirmation. However, when that external confirmation is gone, we fall into a rabbit hole of negative thought patterns that dominate how we feel about ourselves. Within that dark space we begin doubting ourselves. This gives our power back to our inner critic. We belittle ourselves and this makes us feel worthless. Our actions and words start to derive from a place of: I am not enough or I am not loveable enough.

This happens because we don't trust ourselves. We don't trust that whatever we do is good enough. We don't trust that whatever we create is the best we can do. And most importantly, we do not trust that whatever we say or however we behave reflects our best expression. We continually need external confirmation that we are good enough because we don't trust and believe that we actually are.

Very often, deep down in our hearts we know we can do better. We know we can be better. We know we can act better. Yet, over and over again, we don't, and instead we seek confirmation from others that what we are doing is enough. That we are enough.

Yet, most of the time we do not do our best and we know it. We do not step into our greatest potential; we compromise our truest desires and we do not express ourselves fully and authentically. We self-sabotage our words, actions and creations because of the fear buried deep down inside ourselves. Because we do not trust who we are, we fear judgement, rejection and criticism. We start to act out of fear. And when we act out of fear, everything we do turns into a self-fulfilling prophecy. Our fear takes charge of our decisions, our actions and our creations and we start to limit ourselves and run away from who we truly are. Have you ever tried being your absolute best self in full alignment with who you are and still sought the approval of others? You simply do not have to do this if you are happy with yourself; being happy with yourself draws only those to you who see in you their own potential.

Within the fearful mindset, we behave and act in ways that attract the opposite of what we truly desire. We act in the wrong way, we communicate in the wrong way, we make decisions from the wrong places. And we continue to do this to safeguard ourselves from potential suffering. And the worst part is that deep down we know we are moving forward with the handbrake on.

We try to protect ourselves from falling down because we do not trust that we can fly. We do not trust our inner power, our capabilities, our strength and our wisdom. We do things we later regret or feel guilty about because it reinforces our inner fear of loss. Why do we do it? we ask ourselves. We know that acting out of fear brings nothing but more fear to fight. And every fight ignites more inner fight because we are unconsciously afraid of losing what we already have. Sometimes, however, we must lose what we have to receive more of what we truly desire.

Here is the secret: only when we are ready to lose everything are we ready to receive everything. Because no fear of loss will ever allow us to have it all.

When we are ready to lose it all, we stop acting out of fear and we start acting out of trust. We stop pushing away what we truly desire and instead, we start attracting it into our life. When we trust ourselves and follow our desires and dreams we set ourselves free to experience our truest power of creation. We stop belittling ourselves, we open up to receive life's opportunities and we start creating a reality with unlimited possibilities.

When we trust ourselves, we know that whatever we do comes from the best place within ourselves. We need no external recognition, confirmation or validation because we finally recognise and trust ourselves. Self-acceptance is impossible when we act out of fear because it goes against our truest nature – being a creator.

> We can't be the creator if we keep
> acting out of fear, because fear only
> destroys and only love can create.

We have to trust ourselves in order to let go of our fear and start creating a reality in alignment with who we truly are. When we do so, self-acceptance, self-gratitude and self-worth will appear automatically; will be in alignment with our highest self. And that is the only place we can truly create from.

The secret is that when you are truly in alignment with your highest self, you no longer need external approval to prove that you are good enough. You simply accept that you might NOT be good enough and you are okay with that. You love yourself anyway. You let go of trying to be perfect. The pressure you have always put on yourself to prove things to yourself or others suddenly vanishes. You don't have to please anyone any more. You don't have to be liked all the time. In fact, you don't have to do anything in order to feel good with yourself. For the first time, you can simply enjoy experiencing yourself because you know that whatever you do and wherever you are is exactly where you should be. You trust that you are always giving your best with what you have at your disposal at any given moment. This is what self-trust feels like.

If we trust ourselves enough to accept that we are NOT always good enough, we take a bigger step towards self-love than if we are trying to constantly prove otherwise. You see, being okay with our own humanity at any given moment frees us from our own unrelenting expectations. Expectations are rooted in fear and can only bring disappointment. It is when we can see the best in ourselves and others in any situation that we allow ourselves and others to be the best. It is when we trust ourselves enough to welcome every situation as a blessing that we start to feel gratitude for every experience we encounter. And when we feel gratitude for ourselves and life, no matter who we are and where we are, we reconnect with our heart and we step into creating reality from a place of trust.

Thoughts Catcher

Self-criticism is one of the most destructive habits we can have. But there is a simple technique for helping to control your thoughts: become an observer of them. Whenever you catch yourself thinking, consciously categorise your thought. For example:
- Here I am planning.
- Here I am dwelling on the past.
- Here I am worrying about the future.
- Here I am criticising myself.
- Here I am being afraid of something. For example, *I am afraid of not having enough money.*

After you categorise the thought, ask yourself: Who am I? Am I my thoughts? And deliberately let go of it.

Categorising your thoughts in this way will not only help you to spot patterns in your thinking but will also create the necessary distance between you and your thoughts that will allow you to detach from them more easily. Your thoughts, as we have already discussed, are not who you truly are; they are the play of your mind that can get entangled in fear unless you reprogramme it. Your higher self knows who you truly are and by asking yourself this question, you will remind yourself to reconnect with your heart.

19

The Art of Giving and Receiving

We need to stop asking in order
to hear the universe replying.

•

You can't know if you can get something unless you
let go of your desire to have it. Because your desire to
have it is pushing it away from you.

Every one of us likes to receive; but we all experience this want and need differently, and at different times. Some of us at some points seek undivided attention, others prefer adoration. Some of us sometimes want to be seen and heard; at another point we want to be acknowledged and appreciated. Some of us seek care, others affection. But every one of us seeks to receive something in order to feel better about ourselves.

However, if you are not able to give what you crave to receive, you won't be able to create a reality in which you can get what you want. Put another way, if you try to get something that you don't have inside yourself, you will never attract it, you will only repel it and push it away. In order to get it, you have to become it first.

We have a tendency to focus on what we want to receive rather than on how to give. But in that mentality whatever you get is never enough because you are not able to truly receive it either. When we block our giving, we block our receiving as well. And this is why we feel we never have enough, and try to get more and more. As we have looked at already, we create all sorts of techniques and methods to try to force people to give us what we believe we need.

Being a Victim

When we become a victim we try to take and receive from others in order to feel better about ourself. We manipulate people to give us more: we become sick, we tell people we don't feel good, we complain about our circumstances or the past. We try to force people around us to feel sorry for us and to take care of us and give us attention.

We often use our situations and conditions also as an excuse for not giving. We justify our passivity or lack of positive effort by saying we are not well, or blame it on other external circumstances.

The more this technique works on others, the more people start to use it. And if others do give and support, then the person being a victim will probably become more demanding and have higher and higher expectations of others. They will make others feel bad about not taking care of them or not being compassionate enough. They will become unhappy and disappointed with anyone not fulfilling their needs. You see, victims, to 'fill their cup', constantly rely on other people.

A victim's mentality is to take more and more. Their life turns around the question: How much can I get? But, in fact, the opposite will eventually happen. As the victim becomes more and more needy, people slowly start to withdraw from them. This is in part because someone being a victim can't truly appreciate and recognise others or their care; they will just focus on everything they haven't received. This is because they project their own behaviour – of not giving enough – on to you. They will unconsciously make you feel that it is your duty to take care of them and they will punish you for not giving enough while they are not giving anything. They will always find something to complain about. Some people become oppressors and victims at the same time. Those people create difficult, un-beneficial situations in their life so they can become victims of those situations. Of course completely subconsciously!

Manipulation

Another technique to try to force people to give us more is manipulation, which we can also call false giving. This is when your giving is calculated, when you want or expect something back 'in return'. Whether you are giving a compliment, cooking dinner or buying someone a gift, if you do it in order to receive something it is manipulation. You are forcing people to give you something back so that you can feel better about yourself.

When people feel that your giving doesn't come from an honest, authentic, generous place, they are much less likely to give back. And if you haven't received anything for your efforts, the transaction hasn't been made. So you feel unhappy, unrecognised, unappreciated and unsatisfied. You become frustrated, feeling that there is no point in you making those efforts. And you stop your false giving – or you punish the other person for not giving back.

Some people do this by rejecting or distancing themselves from the other person; others become cold or uninterested. Or they may try to make the other person jealous by giving care and attention to someone else instead. But even if this works temporarily, gets someone's attention back for a short time, in the longer term it simply creates insecurity and lack of trust. This kind of relationship can't ever survive.

Both of the techniques mentioned above focus on taking. How can I get what I want? They become not only very addictive but also self-destructive, and keep us away from our deepest desire – unconditional love. Unfortunately, because part of ourselves feels guilty for not being our best self, we end up constantly looking for reassurance and acceptance. We become needy and neediness is the biggest anaphrodisiac. Neediness repulses because it puts pressure on other people. Neediness is nothing else but a belief that we are not a source of our own happiness, fulfilment and joy. It's a belief that we are not a creator of our own reality and therefore rather than to create, we ask to receive.

When we are in the victim mentality or we find ourselves performing manipulation, we are unable to give or to receive and our cup gets emptier and emptier because we are detaching ourselves from our own source of creation. We feel powerless, we stop enjoying life, we create obsessive thoughts about how the world is against us and we try to do anything to distract ourselves from it. We can't see anything else but a negative image of ourselves and our life.

How To Stop Playing the Victim

What shifts the victim mentality is giving itself – true honest giving, without expectations of anything in return. When you start giving you start to create, you become happy with yourself again and your energy changes. You align yourself with who you truly are. You realise that you have the power to fill up your own cup and you claim your own power back. Then others also feel happier with you; so they are more likely to reconnect with you and appreciate you.

True giving is only possible from a place of unconditional love.

How To Respond to Victims

When we can see that someone is practising victim techniques on us, the only good way to respond is not to react to it at all and instead to give appreciation and attention to any positive behaviour the victim shows (like honesty, vulnerability, warmth). After a while, if the technique doesn't work on us, the person will eventually stop using it. If a victim is trying to provoke you, observe without evaluating, don't judge and recognise that you too are capable of being like this, and you will end up feeling compassion towards them. You will be able to see their weaknesses and insecurity, which are mirrors of your own.

Be alert for jealousy. Jealousy only shows up when we are not the best we can be for other people and so feel frightened that someone else might be better for them than us. If you are in your alignment and act from love you will be your best with your partners and friends; you will never get jealous, because you will know that you are giving your best, and you will surrender to the rest. Remember, you can't ever feel secure if your actions come from an insecure place.

Be the Creator

The moral here is that we all sometimes ask to receive love, in one way or another; and we all have victim energy inside ourselves that we sometimes plug into. We forget the creative power we have inside ourselves and we expect the external world to create for us. When we try to exist against our truest nature, however, we suffer and we close up to anything coming our way, feeling more and more empty. What charges us, fulfils us, empowers us and uplifts us is to create. When we create we re-connect to who we truly are. When we create we contribute and give to ourselves, others and life itself. And when we give we open ourselves to fully receive the world around us. We don't need to ask for anything, we simply receive. The energy of asking implies that something is not there yet. It is very different from the energy of receiving, which communicates that whatever you desire, you already have, you already are. In order to receive it, you need to become it first.

The very opposite of a victim is a creator. Be the creator of your life. Today.

Unconditional Giving

This Sunday, cook a meal for a homeless person. It can be something simple; just prepare it with love and offer it to someone who needs it. Giving without wanting something in return is the most powerful expression of unconditional love.

Inner Receiving

Every time you find yourself missing something, longing for something or craving something you are focusing on the lack of that which you desire. And every time you focus on lack of something, speak about lack, think about lack or act out of lack, you create a deficiency in your life. Not only in your life experiences but also within yourself. You feel empty, unfilled, not enough. Every time you focus on what you didn't receive, create, accomplish, experience in your past, you stop yourself creating a different scenario in your reality today. Every time you focus on who you are not, you become less of what you want to be.

Every time you feel unsettled and disappointed with your situation, reflect on the points below.

1. Ask yourself: In which areas of my life am I focusing on deficiency and lack? What do I think I am missing in my life?
2. Out of ten, how much of a deficiency do I feel I have in this area?
3. Now ask yourself: What feelings do I believe this experience will bring me? What feelings do I crave to experience?
4. Think about all the moments from your past when you have experienced those feelings. Bring all those memories and sensations. Feel gratitude for all those experiences you have had and lived. For all the luck you have had to do everything you've done, have everything you've had, be everything you are, and experience everything you've experienced in your life. Do you see now that you do have inside you a whole universe of the feeling you were craving? You just have to see it in you, acknowledge it and appreciate it. Gratitude is the very essence of wholeness, fulfilment and abundance.
5. Check again within yourself: out of ten, how much of a deficiency do you feel now?
6. Every time you catch yourself focusing on what you have not experienced, ask yourself instead: What have I experienced that I liked? How many people do not have a chance to experience that? Can I be grateful for what I have received and created so far?

20

Wholeness

We are all fractured and this life is our
opportunity to assemble all the pieces of
our soul to become a whole again.

•

The only true freedom is love.

I was born a whole. Then life circumstances fractured me. I have
dedicated my life to reassembling myself again.

In the last chapters we looked at how we all crave love and attention and how we are ready to push, manipulate, provoke and fight
for it – as well as be ready and to run away when we think that we are
not getting enough of it. The aim of this constant hunt for love and
validation from others is to fill up the emptiness within ourselves.

For me myself, I did not receive enough love as a child; therefore I
not only had no idea what receiving enough love looks and feels like,
but also, I would always focus on the lack of love in my life rather
than the existence of love. My damaged perspective would always
search for proof that I was not loved by others, rather than acknowledging proof of the love I was receiving. You see, our disempowering
beliefs always want proof of warped thinking to validate our pain.

I felt not enough within myself and no external situation
could ever make me feel otherwise. Quite the opposite – and
we have looked at this idea previously – I would subconsciously
attract circumstances and relationships into my life that would
prove me right; that what I already believed was true.

Whatever You Believe is Always True

As Henry Ford said: 'If you think you can do a thing or think you can't do a thing, you're right.' Your reality will always adjust to match what you believe and how you perceive yourself. So, if you believe you are not loveable, people around you will treat you accordingly until you fully experience what 'not being loveable' feels like. For me, for many years I believed that I wasn't good enough, and thus I always sought reasons to substantiate my thinking. Why? Because I never chose to believe otherwise.

Experience the Opposite

As Neale Donald Walsch says: 'You cannot experience yourself as what you are until you've encountered what you are not. This is the purpose of the theory of relativity, and all physical life. It is by that which you are not that you yourself are defined.'[33]

We can't ever experience the positive without experiencing the negative. We cannot know ourselves as rich until we become aware of poor. We cannot create ourselves until we un-create ourselves. Or, put another way, we can only truly experience what loveable means if we know its opposite. This is the Law of Opposites. Every time you experience yourself as lacking in something, you open the window to experience yourself as the exact opposite. It means that you have created the necessary context for the antithesis to manifest itself when you are ready.

From this angle, every 'negative' experience is an opportunity for the 'positive' experience to be created. Therefore, don't resist negative experiences, don't punish yourself for limiting beliefs, don't mull over your failures and don't dwell on past events that brought you pain; those experiences were created as a chance for you to experience their opposite. When you resist accepting negative situations, you also resist the positive opposite coming into your life. Therefore, view every negative experience as a signal that future positive experience can now emerge. If you truly desire something, in order for this to be created in your life you must first know its opposite.

Experience Wholeness

Ask yourself, what have you experienced yourself as not? Not good enough, not loveable enough, not abundant enough, not worthy enough, not important enough, not powerful enough?

Enough of lack, enough of deficiency! You have now enough context to create yourself as the very opposite of that! You are ready to become wholeness now!

Let go of your unpleasant past events, let go of your sad memories, let go of your negative beliefs and simply realise that you have now gathered enough experience to finally know what 'ENOUGH' feels like.

You are one decision away from changing completely the direction of your life. Simply realise: You are ready. You have suffered enough, you have doubted yourself enough, you have done enough not loving yourself, you have been unkind to yourself enough, you have been a victim enough, you have been afraid enough... it is enough luck now.

You are now ready to become the creator you perhaps always knew you were. Simply choose today to stop resisting and rejecting all those negative experiences and start to finally use them as a possibility to create the opposite – the wholeness.

Choose today to be loveable enough, worthy enough, kind to yourself enough, in love with life enough, abundant enough, joyful enough and whatever else your heart wishes to experience next. You are it, already. And when you see that you are it, you will start to behave as it, you will start to create as it, you will start to attract and manifest as it.

Remember, everything starts from us.

The greatest love you can ever receive is the love that comes from knowing that you are love.

Learn to love all your lucks, all your fears, all your anger and guilt, and before you know it, it will all melt away and create an opportunity for its opposite to come to fruition. Don't resist it. The more you fight yourself and delve into your deficiencies, the more you become a prisoner of them.

Realise and remember that the purpose of any negative experience, of any negative feeling, is not to persist in your life but to only give you a context in which to create its very opposite experience.

When you choose to become love, you love everything that you feel at every moment, you stop breaking apart your own love and you unite again, into a whole.

You are whole. You are love.

Self-Celebration

Today I want you to celebrate your new self. Invite your friends over, cook a delicious meal, treat yourself with a massage. Whatever a celebration means to you. Be proud of everything that you have become.

And over the next week, every day do something that is proof of your new self. If you have finally decided to be loveable, do something that proves it. If you have finally decided to be worthy or good enough, do something that proves that. And keep doing it – because this is who you truly are.

Oh, and lastly, when you wake up tomorrow, write yourself a love letter. What is it that you appreciate about yourself, what is it that you love about yourself? What is it that you are proud of?

21

The Final Message

If you have been given a dream or a desire, it means
that you have everything in yourself to achieve it.

·

When we are willing to let go of our identity, let go of
our control and become lost, merged, blended and
united with someone, we are allowing ourselves to find
ourselves again, to recognise and to re-create
ourselves from a new, fuller and richer whole.

·

Sometimes we need to turn our head from
what is dying towards what is coming alive.

There is no good or bad way, there is simply the way we take. We live to feel, experience, witness and create. Each way teaches us something, helps us discover something. It may happen that we spend many years following the 'wrong' ways, being in the 'wrong' places, before we eventually recognise the right way for us. Sometimes life does not bring us what we ask for, because we don't know how to ask for it. And sometimes we need to stop asking in order to hear the universe replying. Life gives us, however, people, experiences and situations that are helpful for discovering who we are. If we are not able to understand the situation the first time, similar situations will repeat until we grasp it. It may take some time.

It is amazing how often people repeat the same patterns in life and expect different results. It's like making the same salad, with the same ingredients, and expecting it to taste different.

It is essential to experiment, try, discover and learn. To find out what really lights us up and to realise our potential. What is beautiful about the past is that it shows what we do not want to take with us into the future. We often want new things in our life but we don't want our life to change. But we need to welcome change. If you pray for the new, be ready for it to appear in your life and to receive it.

Our life script hasn't been written down. We are here to write it. And sometimes we need to learn how to destroy before we learn how to create. We need to learn how to un-create ourselves before we can give ourselves a new form and a new experience. We need to unlearn how to look at things and learn how to see them.

There are no good or bad experiences. There are simply experiences, and it is through them that we become closer to ourselves and discover who we really are. Let us refrain from judging, evaluating or criticising ourselves for the wrong choices we've made. Every experience is important and it has its role and purpose. It is designed to teach us something, make us discover something, guide us or allow us to create its opposite. Every new experience becomes a new substance to create with. Create who you are and create from who you are.

Whoever and whatever you desire to attract, become it. This attitude changes everything, for there is no better love than self-love. And the most beautiful things you can ever receive are those you can give to yourself. Let us fall in love with ourselves. For good and bad. Let's forgive ourselves for all of our mistakes. Let's accept our own imperfections. Let's not set any conditions for when and how we will love ourselves.

And self-love is accepting not only all parts of ourselves, but also all the aspects of ourselves mirrored through other people. Rather than being hard on ourselves for everything that we are not, let's celebrate everything that we are. Seeing, understanding and loving everything as part of a whole might not be simple. Yet without darkness there wouldn't be light. And without sadness, there wouldn't be happiness. We wouldn't be able to recognise it.

Happiness is not getting what you want but wanting what you get. You don't have to be good at anything in order to be happy. When you are happy, no matter what you do it is done right, because it's done from the heart. When you are happy with yourself for everything that you are, you will attract plenty of joy and magic into your life. When you change how you perceive yourself, your whole reality changes. When you stop telling yourself one story, another emerges. The more love and acceptance you give your flaws, the less visible they will become. And, people will only ever treat you according to how you treat yourself. Let go of everything you are not and become everything that you are. Sometimes we need to turn our head from what is dying towards what is coming alive.

We grow to better serve life, to serve love and to offer a contribution that is unique to us. Every person holds their own beauty and has a particular expression to fulfil on the path of life. Every single person is unique and different; there is no one else in this world just like you, and that means that there is no one else you can possibly compare yourself to. In other words, your unique self, with your unique expression, your unique laugh, your unique sensitivity and your unique perception, must be perfect the way it is, because another person like you simply doesn't exist. Discover all parts of yourself and express them all fully. Leave behind the need for external validation and learn to validate yourself. Sometimes we need a push from life – to break down, to come apart, to be disassembled, to un-become and to un-create ourselves so that we can come together in a new, bigger, bolder form, to move forward.

Being in a Low Mood and Feeling Unloveable

When we are in an elevated mood we feel happy, joyful, fulfilled and satisfied. We energetically communicate: 'I am loveable', because this is how we feel. We like ourselves. We are happy with ourselves. We desire ourselves. However, when we are in a low mood, we send out the polar opposite information: 'I am not loveable'. And these are the moments in which we often expect other people to reassure us that we are wrong and to raise our spirits. The problem is, if this is how we feel about ourselves, then more than likely we will behave in an unloveable way. We might be grumpy, angry, mean. People may just want to stay out of our way, to not do anything that will upset us even more. And of course, this is the last thing we truly desire. So we start looking for all sorts of problems. Our mind, not used to simply sitting with negative emotions, tries to find a reason for them to justify and solve them. All we are doing is projecting on our relationships our current inner state. In this state, we perceive our reality through dark, moody and smudged lenses.

The most important thing to do when we are in a low mood is to recognise it before we react to anything. We must accept that this life comes with waves of emotions and we need to be gentle with ourselves. Treat yourself in the same way you would treat your best friend. Give yourself a healthy dose of attention, recognition and care.

It often helps to look at yourself in the third person.
- What does this person need right now?
- What advice would you give this person?

If you have to withdraw from friends, partners, social life generally, do it. But it is important to communicate to people around you how you feel to give them a chance to take care of you before you push them away. Understand that low moods happen to everyone and often they have nothing to do with what is going on in our life. They might be hormonal or caused by inadequate sleep, or any number of other things. Whatever the reason, remember that after every storm the sun will rise again. You will eventually feel better.

Being Trapped in One Upsetting Situation

When you find yourself trapped in one negative thought process, it is very important to remember to always take a broader perspective on the situation. My favourite term is: 'ZOOM OUT', by which I mean adjust your perspective to focus on the whole situation, not the detail. Most of the problems we perceive or fight with others about are not real problems but just reactions to certain situations and behaviours that have triggered us. We take things personally when they are personal. Which means, they often do not have much to do with someone else's behaviour but are about our own perception of it and the meaning we are giving to it. As we have seen, we experience our reality through a filter of the beliefs we have about others and ourselves. Those beliefs come from our experiences, and the same thing will keep triggering us over and over again until we give it a different meaning.

Remember: How we perceive something depends on the angle we are looking at it from. Within the palm of our hands we hold the power to control how we perceive our reality. Become reflective, not reactive. The most effective way to practise this is to 'ZOOM OUT' from every situation that triggers us, and to look at it from an outside perspective and come up with at least a few possible different interpretations. Once we prove to ourselves that there is no one defined interpretation that is the ultimate truth, we can simply see that we may not be right about our version of it. It is also worth asking: Is this a 'real' problem or am I creating the problem now?

One of the most beautiful pieces of advice I have had, from a dear friend, was this. If you are upset about something someone has said or done, ask yourself: Am I going to be upset about it for longer than ten minutes? If the answer is no, then don't bring it up. If the answer is yes then ask yourself another question: Am I going to be upset about it for longer than one hour? If the answer is no, then drop it. If the answer is yes, then ask yourself the last question: Am I going to be upset about it in three days' time? If the answer is no, then let go. If the answer is yes, then wait a day to calm down and then talk about it with a healthier twenty-four-hour perceptive.

Don't have a conversation about every detail. Just ask yourself: can I accept it or can I honestly not live with it? Then make a decision about whether you truly want to bring it up. Remember: as long as what we feel for each other doesn't change, the events don't matter. The best perspective is to always assume that everything is just fine. Often when we Zoom Out, look at our entire life and remind ourselves what we are here to do in this life and who we truly are, we will realign and reconnect with our highest selves and the negative perspective will fade away.

When You Are Not Sure What to Do, Act Out of Love

Whatever you do, always act out of love. Many of our actions come from self-protective mechanisms, fear of rejection, of judgement, of abandonment and so many other fears. And always remember, whatever you do out of fear will bring nothing else but more fear to fight with. The outcome of any situation that was created out of fear cannot be positive; it will simply lead to exactly what you are afraid of. When we act out of love, by contrast, we not only create the best possible outcome for ourselves but we also raise our self-worth. Self-love and self-acceptance are impossible when we act out of fear, because acting out of fear is a rejection of our power of creation.

When we act out of love, self-acceptance, self-gratitude, self-worth and self-esteem appear instantaneously because we are now in alignment with our truest nature and our highest potential. It is the only place we can truly create anything from. External input does not add to our value; our own sense of self-worth and self-gratitude do that. And if we act out of fear, our value is diminished. Every time you want to act, ask yourself: Is this coming out of love, or out of fear? And act accordingly. Only when we are ready to lose everything are we ready to receive everything. Because the fear of loss will never allow us to have it all.

Never Assume You Are Right

Never assume that you are 'right'. The disappointment we experience in any situation comes from our beliefs about it. Our beliefs about what is right or what is wrong. But every single person has slightly different beliefs. What is normal for me might be unfamiliar to you. We assume that only when we will receive what we believe is right for us will we be happy. But what if being happy is not getting what we want but wanting what we get?

If you look for problems, you will find them; if you look for what is not working, you will find that. To give anything a chance, assume that you don't know what is right or wrong for you and be open to discovering yourself all over again in every situation.

Sometimes when everything is going well in our life, we still manage to find things to complain about because this is how we have been programmed. Our mind, as we have seen, has a tendency to focus on the negative. Your thoughts, however, only have power over you if you believe them.

When You Don't Know How to Communicate

Communication is so important! We are constantly creating our reality with everything we say. We often have a tendency to create self-fulfilling prophecies. We tend to focus on what we assume is not working, forgetting to praise what is. With other people, we often point out what we 'never' do together, rather than asking or taking the initiative to create them. We communicate our doubts and differences rather than sharing our security, reassurance or appreciation. With this kind of negative communication, we sadly discourage any friendship or relationship from blooming. Therefore, first stop talking to your friends about your problems. When you focus on the problem you are blocking the chances of the condition improving. The vibration of your problem is so loud that you can't allow what you want instead. Make it less loud. Don't speak about it, don't think about it. Stop trying. Stop manipulating. Just stay aligned. Don't try to make it happen, allow it to happen. Get to the place of pure appreciation. Everything you want is coming to you. All you have to want is to be in the vibrational place to recognise it when it comes.

Think about what you want instead of what you don't want. If you don't know what you want, how can you ask for it? What would change if you started to point out and share all the good things about your relationships, about your partner or your friends and family? Never point to the other person, always focus on yourself, because it is you who has the power to influence and change your reality according to what you believe about it. Focus on your own feelings rather than someone else's. Very often in our relationships, we have a tendency to try to figure out what the other person is feeling and thinking. The truth is, it is not your business. If they would like you to know they will communicate that. The most important thing is that you know what it is that you are feeling. Are you connected to yourself enough to meet your feelings where they are at? Often when we feel insecure, instead of asking for reassurance we make the other person feel insecure as well. But if you make someone else feel insecure, they will never be able to reassure you.

When You are Not Happy with Where You Are

Assume that all is always perfect and every situation serves your greatest good. If someone doesn't have time for you, maybe you are supposed to use this time differently. Life always wants the best for you. Perhaps you need some alone time to reflect or create some new ideas or recharge and nourish yourself. If you are in a situation that frustrates you, remind yourself that every situation has something to offer if only you are open to receive it.

If something you have planned has been cancelled and you are disappointed, remember that you don't know if the situation you were hoping for would turn out the way you imagined it. Maybe not. Perhaps life was protecting you from something. Everything comes from you and is good for you.

If you are somewhere you don't want to be, ask yourself: *How can I take this situation in my life and create the best out of it? What can I do to make that moment the best ever?*

Whatever you do, try not to wait for anything. Don't be in the past, of what has not happened, or in the future, waiting for something better to come. Focus on what is here and now. What can you do to make this moment ideal? Put your heart into everything you do. Celebrate every moment. Relish every activity (even if it is the washing-up).

When we learn to be here and now, not only with ourselves but also with each other, that is where the real magic happens.

When You Feel Sad and Alone

If you are feeling alone it often means you are not getting the attention you desire. The cure for that is simple: give yourself attention.

Remember, other people can't give you what they don't have. If your partner or a friend or family member is not being affectionate nor loving, don't assume that this is because you are not loveable. It is because at this moment in time they just don't have any love to give. If you are feeling alone – fill up your own cup. An empty cup is nothing else but a lack of appreciation and attention. In our relationships with others, as we have seen, we often blame the other person for how we feel; but the truth is that no one has the power to make you feel anything. If I ask you to get angry now, can you do it for me? No. Because you have no 'reason' to. In the same way, someone can't make us feel something, they cannot fill our cup. We can only ever fill it ourselves, with the right attitude and beliefs about ourselves.

When our cup is full, we often receive the appreciation and recognition from other people automatically, because they can see how well we are. Have you noticed that it is often couples where both people are driven by their own passions and move forward in the same direction who are the happiest? It's because they are both self-sufficient. They get their satisfaction from what they do and who they are and they bring that beautiful energy back home. They don't rely on the other person to fulfil their needs, they do it themselves. They are their own support system.

How to fill up your cup? Ask yourself, what is it that you love and appreciate yourself for? What is it that you do that makes you feel alive, inspired and proud of yourself? And now, simply take some time to do it every day. Get your own dose of self-love every day and you will never have to ask for it from other people, it will be there automatically. When you like yourself, people will also like you. When you are passionate about something, when you are in your own element, you become more confident and inspiring. You become more desirable. When you are in your element you don't 'need' your partner, family or friends. And it is the energy of need that blocks desire. Esther Perel says what builds desire is this: When we laugh together, when we break the routine, when we are apart from each other and when we are passionate about something. Let's stop using people for our reason to feel better or worse. Let's choose to feel good in every moment.[34]

When You Are Anxious

Be playful. Play and anxiety don't go together. When you are anxious you can't be playful, you can't experience pure connection and pleasure or creativity.

Be present. Most of our worries are not about today but tomorrow. And you don't know what tomorrow might bring. You may get a new job, a new house or a new opportunity. Everything might change. Don't assume you know what tomorrow will look like, it's impossible. If you are not fully present in everything you do, you will never feel that you did it well. In relationships, take them day by day! If staying in your relationship is working for you today, then enjoy it fully. And have fun in the process. Commit to every day.

I Am Ready for a Relationship; How Can I Attract It?

Are you truly ready to open up for your next relationship? Have you done everything you wanted to do before settling down with someone? Sometimes you can only build togetherness once you have learned how to be with yourself. If you are single and would like to attract a perfect partner, assume that this person will show up in the next six months. It's done. It's happening. What are all the things you might want to do before you meet this person? The things you can only do by yourself? Stop asking for your dream partner every day and start to do it all today.

When we keep asking for something we can't receive it, as the energy of receiving is very different from the energy of asking. When we keep asking for something, we communicate from a place of luck and therefore we keep pushing it away. When we let go and just assume that something is happening, we are ready to receive it.

The energy that communicates that something is done is the energy of gratitude, as we are only grateful for things that have happened already.

Ask yourself: *How it would feel in my body if my partner was already next to me, right now? How differently would I feel about myself? How differently would I speak, act and think?* Bring that energy into your field as often as possible and change your vibration accordingly. When you wake up, when you're driving, when you're eating your dinner... and be **grateful** for it.

When You Feel Unloveable

Stop controlling love. People don't love us for what we do but for who we are. There is nothing you have to do to deserve to be loved. Some people believe that the harder one has to work for love, the more worthy the other person is of it. If you believe that you are loved for what you do then you will always feel you haven't done enough, and you might blame yourself for it. We all deserve to be loved just as we are for no other reason than the joy of loving.

You might be thinking, 'Well, all this is not that easy in my situation.' So, I'll pose a question: 'Is there anybody on Earth who was in the same situation and made their own dreams come true?'

The answer is yes.

So, what's stopping you? If you have been given a dream or a desire, it means that you have everything in yourself to achieve it.

Remember one thing: if you are not sure that something is impossible, there is a chance – often a higher chance than you believe – that it's feasible. If you do not know what is feasible in life, assume that everything is. Always. The only way to invest in your future is to create it now.

Notes

1 Catto, Jamie, *Insanely Gifted*. Canongate Books, 2016
2 Hilbig, B., 'Good things don't come easy (to mind): explaining framing effects in judgments of truth', *Experimental Psychology*. 2011; 59(1):38–46. doi: 10.1027/1618-3169/a000124
3 Beattie, Melody, *Codependent No More*. Hazelden Publishing, 1986
4 en.wikipedia.org/wiki/Cognitive_dissonance
5 Cooley, C.H., *Human Nature and the Social Order*. Scribner, 1922
6 Jung, C.G., *Psychology and Religion*. Yale University Press, 1960
7 goodreads.com/book/show/55778608-the-shadow-getting-to-know-your-darker-half
8 Catto, *Insanely Gifted*
9 Odoul, Michel, *What Your Aches and Pains Are Telling You*. Healing Arts Press, 2018
10 Richo, David, *How to Be an Adult: A Handbook on Psychological and Spiritual Integration*. Paulist Press, 1991
11 Jung, C.G., *Psychology and Alchemy*. Princeton University Press, 1980
12 Richo, *How to Be an Adult*
13 Dispenza, Joe, *Becoming Supernatural: How Common People Are Doing The Uncommon*. Hay House, 2017
14 Charbonnier, André, *Plus de peurs que de mal (It Could Have Been Worse)*. Editions Points, Paris, 2016

15 Kübler-Ross, Elisabeth, *On Death and Dying: What the Dying Have to Teach Doctors, Nurses, Clergy and Their Own Families*. Scribner, 1969

16 Walsch, Neale Donald, *Conversations with God*. Hodder & Stoughton, 1997

17 Ouspensky, Peter, *In Search of the Miraculous*. Paul H. Crompton Ltd, 2014

18 Berceli, David, *Un Uomo Fatto D'argilla: Aiutami a Guarire me Stesso. (A Man Made of Clay: Help Me to Heal Myself)*. Via Magna Grecia, Rome, 2011

19 Seigel, M (2021) *Enhanced States of Consciousness* in collaboration with Mindvalley. Interviewed by Dorota Stańczyk

20 Bean, Orson, *Too Much Is Not Enough*. Lyle Stuart, 1988

21 Sparks, Nicholas, *At First Sight*. Grand Central Publishing, 2006

22 Jenett, Marilyn, *Feel Free to Prosper: Two Weeks to Unexpected Income with the Simplest Prosperity Laws Available*. Tarcherperigee, 2015

23 Tracy, Brian, *Maximum Achievement*. Simon & Schuster, 1995

24 Murphy, Joseph, *The Power of Your Subconscious Mind*. Penguin, 2011

25 Charbonnier, *Plus de peurs que de mal (It Could Have Been Worse)*

26 Kaptchuk, T., 'The power of the placebo effect', www.health.harvard.edu/mental-health/the-power-of-the-placebo-effect, 9 August 2019

27 Murphy, *The Power of Your Subconscious Mind*

28 ibid

[29] Perel, Esther, *The State of Affairs: Rethinking Infidelity.* Yellow Kite, 2017

[30] twitter.com/estherperel/status/563054510906830851?lang=en

[31] twitter.com/babaramdass/status/955850195350315008?lang=en

[32] Schützenberger, Ancelin, *The Ancestor Syndrome: Transgenerational Psychotherapy and the Hidden Links in the Family Tree.* Routledge, 1998

[33] Walsch, *Conversations with God*

[34] rekindlingdesire.estherperel.com/sign-up

Further Reading

Berceli, David, *Zaufaj Ciału*. Wydawnictwo Ośrodek Bioenergetycznej Pracy z Ciałem, Pomocy i Edukacji Psychologicznej, 2011

Catto, Jamie, *Insanely Gifted*. Canongate Books, 2016

Chapman, Gary, *The 5 Love Languages: The Secret to Love that Lasts*. Northfield Publishing, Chicago, 1995

Charbonnier, André, *Plus de Peurs Que de Mal (It Could Have Been Worse)*. Editions Points, Paris, 2016

Dispenza, Joe, *Becoming Supernatural: How Common People Are Doing the Uncommon*. Hay House, 2017

Fitzsimmons, Terrance W., *Leadership Quarterly*. Elsevier Inc., The University of Queensland, 2013

Ford, Debbie, *The Best Year of Your Life*. HarperCollins, 2004

Freedom Long, Max, *The Secret Science at Work*. Medium Publishing House, 1996

Gawdat, Mo, *Solve for Happy: Engineer Your Path to Joy*. Gallery Books, 2017

Gottman, John M., Gottman, Julie Carlton, Abrams, Rachel, *The Man's Guide to Women*. Rodale Books, 2016

Gladwell, Malcolm, *Blink: The Power of Thinking Without Thinking*. Back Bay Books, 2007

Gungor, Mark, *Laugh Your Way to a Better Marriage*. Atria Books, 2009

Hawkins, David R., *Letting Go: The Pathway of Surrender*. Hay House, 2014

Hesse, Herman, *Siddhartha*. Penguin Classics, 2008

Jenett, Marilyn, *Feel Free to Prosper*. Tarcher, 2015

Kübler-Ross, Elisabeth, *On Death and Dying*. Scribner, 1969

Martel, Jacques, *The Complete Dictionary of Ailments and Diseases*. Les Éditions ATMA Internationales, Quebec, 1998

Murphy, Joseph, *The Power of Your Subconscious Mind*. Simon & Schuster, 2019

Odoul, Michel, *Tell Me Where It Hurts And I'll Tell You Why*. Les Éditions Albin Michel, Paris, 2013

Osho, *The Book of Man*. Czarna Owca Publishing House, Warsaw, 2014

Ouspensky, Peter Demianovich, *In Search of the Miraculous Fragments of an Unknown Teaching*. Czarna Owca Publishing House, Warsaw, 2010

Perel, Esther, *The State of Affairs: Rethinking Infidelity*. Yellow Kite, 2019

Pransky, George S., *The Relationship Handbook*. Pransky and Associates, 2017

Renaud, Gilbert, *Recall Healing. Healing Through Awareness*. Wena Publishing House, 2013

Ruiz, Don Miguel, *The Four Agreements: A Practical Guide to Personal Freedom*. Éditions Jouvence, Saint Julien en Genevois Cedex, 2016

Sharma, Robin, *Discover Your Destiny*. Jaico Books, 2014

Singer, Michael A., *The Untethered Soul. New Harbinger*, 2007

Singer, Michael A., *The Surrender Experiment, My Journey into Life's Perfection*. Yellow Kite, 2016

Tracy, Brian, *Maximum Achievement*. Simon & Schuster, 1995

Walsch, Neale Donald, *Conversations with God*, Hodder & Stoughton, 1997

Zukav Gary, Francis Linda, *Thoughts from the Heart of the Soul*. Free Press Publishing House, 2002

Acknowledgements

Many people contributed to my growth; I owe my gratitude to so many mentors and teachers. However, the most important person I would like to thank is myself for not giving up, for trusting, continuing to do the work, and believing. I first started writing this book nine years ago. I completed the first version in Polish, which I translated to English, and then threw it away. The first version was all about relationships; I realised that I could not write about relationships before fully exploring and understanding the most crucial relationship in my life – the one I had with myself. Around four years ago, I started to work on the second version of my book in English, and this book is the result.

I was writing most of it for myself. The realisations, ideas, exercises and methods I was learning, discovering and creating were helping me daily to re-create myself and my life. When some of the realisations were enlightening to me, it was so overwhelming that I could not go to sleep until I had written it all down. I am beyond grateful that I can now share this wisdom with you.

I want to thank my parents and my brother for being the most influential teachers in my life. I want to thank every one of my romantic partners, who are all incredible humans and who I will always keep in my heart. You were my mirror and you showed me the most hidden, unseen, rejected parts of myself. My journey of self-love would not be possible without those relationships.

I want to thank all my friends, those who have left my life and those who stayed. Every person was significant. They either pushed me to learn to love myself unconditionally or taught me how to be unconditionally loved. You know who you are!

Lastly, I would like to thank all my guardians, guides, teachers, mentors, collaborators and all other unique humans on the same mission of making this world a more loving and peaceful place. Neale Donald Walsch, for being my dear friend and teacher. Your wisdom has truly changed my life! Mo Gawdat, for all your support, your faith in me, your friendship and your trust. I truly hope we will make 1 billion people happier! Ajahn Luongta Saiyut, for teaching me awareness and meditation. You have opened my eyes to see my inner world for the very first time. Sherab Gyaltsen Rinpoche, for your blessing and your refuge. That moment initiated one of the most important changes in my life. Vitorio and Evia, my spiritual guides, for always showing me what I could not see myself and guiding me towards unconditional love. Marie Diamond, for being my mentor and guardian angel for the last five years. Vishen Lakhiani, for changing my world and teaching me what is possible to create in this life. Oz Garcia, for your wisdom, knowledge and always being there for me, my dear friend. Lisa Nichols and Eric Edmeades for teaching me about the art of self-confidence and public speaking. Joe Dispenza, for expanding my mind and my heart. Nassim Haramein, for enriching and expanding my perception of this reality. Lawrence Bloom, rest in peace, for helping me gather all the broken pieces of my soul. I am sure there are many people I forgot to list, but the names I have mentioned are people I have met who have significantly impacted how I perceive the world and myself. Thank you all again!

About the Author

Dorota Stańczyk is a Polish transformational artist, creative director, public speaker, conscious creativity trainer and entrepreneur. Dorota combines her knowledge of creativity and consciousness to design digital products, transformational events and experiences in the wellness industry. Her passion is to combine fine arts, personal growth and interactive technology to raise awareness of new models and paradigms of living, working and being.

Dorota completed her studies at the world-renowned Duperré School of Applied Arts in Paris. She worked for over 10 years in Visual Arts, combining digital and physical arts to conceptualise services and create innovative designs and projects. As the Executive Creative Director of Mindvalley for two years, Dorota applied her knowledge to support innovative learning approaches and led a 30+ people team of filmmakers, designers, writers and content marketing specialists. She has worked with authors and influencers such as: Wim Hof, Jason Silva, Steven Kotler, Michael Beckwith, Neale Donald Walsch, Lisa Nichols, Jim Kwick, Russell Simmons, Nassim Haramein, Vishen Lakhiani, Gelong Thubten, Dave Asprey, Nicole Bradford, Mo Gawdat, Erick Edmeades, Srikumar Rao, Marisa Peer, Donna Eden and more.

In December 2019, Dorota created INNERART Ltd – Transformational Arts Consultancy Agency, which advises on creating digital products, events and spaces in the wellness industry that merge art, technology and personal growth. Her clients include Sensie App and Uptime, the self-described 'knowledge hacking' app that raised $16 million in seed funding, after officially launching on iOS in January 2020. In 2020, Dorota co-founded Appii App with Mo Gawdat, the former chief business officer for Google X and author of *Solve For Happy*. Appii is a personal happiness app that uses data science and AI to track your mood and curate personalised recommendations for exercises and expert advice on happiness.

Dorota also worked on a full-length documentary on Enhanced States of Consciousness in collaboration with Mindvalley and published numerous articles on self-awareness, creativity and innovation. She is currently working on another documentary movie series on Hacking Happiness. *(Re)Create Yourself* is her first book.

Download the Appii app in Apple's app store, Google's play store or go to www.appii.app. Use the promo code [Recreateyourself] to receive 3 months premium subscription for free.

Follow Dorota on social media:

 @dorotastanczykart

 dorota.art

 @dorota_stanczyk

To receive Dorota's latest articles, musings and news regarding any upcoming events, trainings, workshops and online courses subscribe to her newsletter at:
www.dorotastanczyk.com

books to help you live a good life

Join the conversation and tell
us how you live a #goodlife

🐦 @yellowkitebooks
f YellowKiteBooks
📌 Yellow Kite Books
📷 YellowKiteBooks